THE
HEALING
JOURNEY
THROUGH JOB LOSS

Your Journal for
Reflection and Revitalization

Phil Rich, EdD, MSW
Stuart A. Copans, MD
Kenneth G. Copans, CPA

John Wiley & Sons, Inc.

NEW YORK ✦ CHICHESTER ✦ WEINHEIM ✦ BRISBANE ✦ SINGAPORE ✦ TORONTO

This book is printed on acid-free paper. ∞

Copyright © 1999 by Phil Rich, Stuart A. Copans, and Kenneth G. Copans.

Published by John Wiley & Sons, Inc.

Published simultaneously in Canada.

The Healing Journey™ is a trademark of John Wiley & Sons, Inc.

This publication is designed to provide accurate and authoritative information in regard to the subject matter covered. It is sold with the understanding that the publisher is not engaged in rendering professional services. If legal, accounting, medical, psychological, or any other expert assistance is required, the services of a competent professional person should be sought.

Library of Congress Cataloging-in-Publication Data:
Rich, Phil.
    The healing journey through job loss : your journal for reflection and revitalization / Phil Rich, Stuart A. Copans, and Kenneth G. Copans.
      p.   cm.
  Includes bibliographical references.
  ISBN 0-471-32694-1 (paper : alk. paper)
   1. Unemployment—Psychological aspects.   2. Career changes—Psychological aspects.   1. Copans, Stuart.   II. Copans, Kenneth G.   III. Title.
  HD5708.R53 1999   98-56175
  650.14—dc21   CIP

Printed in the United States of America.
10 9 8 7 6 5 4 3 2 1

Contents

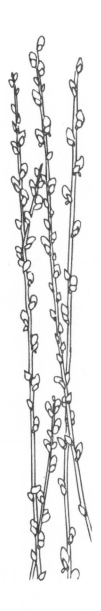

About *The Healing Journey Through Job Loss*

WE'VE SEEN MANY changes in the work environment over the past decade and beyond. There have been multiple layoffs as companies have "downsized," "rightsized," and "reconfigured." There's also been a major change in the basic work "contract" that once existed between employer and employee. Jobs that were once secure for life, with all the fiscal benefits, now rarely exist. The social contract that guaranteed employment and told you what you could expect is gone. People entering the workforce today are likely to change employers and jobs multiple times over their working careers.

In all industries, the employee—from line worker through senior administrator—has taken pay cuts, lost benefits, assumed increased workloads, or has been laid off. Some people have never been able to find equivalent positions and so have taken dramatic cuts in pay and authority, or even switched industries or careers completely. More experienced workers have been pushed out one way or another, replaced by younger or part-time employees, or not at all.

With all these changes in the larger industrial environment, it's no wonder that the very *idea* of job security has become almost nonexistent.

The Healing Journey Through Job Loss is a book about the effects of job loss on your life. It's *not* a book about why people lose their jobs, or how to find a new one. There are plenty of books available to help you prepare a resume, develop a network, explore your interests, figure out your finances, and create new career paths, many of which are excellent resources. *The Healing Journey Through Job Loss* will help with the *emotional* tasks of recovery and renewal as you face the reality (financially, practically, and emotionally) of losing your job. Research data suggest that the chances for reemployment are improved for those people who deal with the emotional issues that surround unemployment.

Whatever the circumstances of your job loss—whether recently fired or long out of work—it is important to work through its effects on your life. *The Healing Journey Through Job Loss* is a guided journal that will help you make sense of the effects of losing your job on your life and sense of identity. In it you'll find a place to express your thoughts and find your own answers as you regain your footing along your life journey. As a journal, *The Healing Journey Through Job Loss* can serve as a valuable record of your life at this difficult time and provide a way to work through your sense of loss, reflect on your feelings, and find ways to rebuild your life ahead.

I

Embarking on Your Journey

"All things fall and are built again."
—WILLIAM BUTLER YEATS

THE HEALING JOURNEY through job loss begins when you get your pink slip. For many, it's probably an unexpected journey and one you certainly don't want to embark upon. You may feel as though you've been kicked in the stomach or thrown overboard in a storm.

Of course, many people lose their jobs each day for many different reasons. For some, job loss is the result of poor performance or lack of aptitude for the work. For an increasing number of people, job loss is the result of organizational and industry-wide redesign and layoffs. For these employees, job loss is typically not the consequence of poor work, but the result of a far removed executive decision to cut back on staff, replacing them one way or another with someone who can do the job better, more effectively, more efficiently, and/or—above all—more cheaply.

When job loss takes this route, the result is not only loss of work but a sense of disappointment, unfairness, surprise, and anger. The very concept of a fair day's wage for a fair day's job is challenged, and people walk away with a sense of having been used, treated unfairly, and disregarded. Adding insult to injury for many of these people, expressions such as "reduction in work force," "downsizing" or "rightsizing," and "layoff" are simply euphemisms that politely rephrase the fact that you've just been fired and lost your livelihood.

This personal journal can be a comforting and illuminating companion in your recovery from job loss.

Keeping a Journal

If you're reading this book, the chances are you've been laid off or lost your job for reasons other than the quality of your work. *The Healing Journey Through Job Loss* can help you come to terms with and work through your situation by helping you explore your loss, identify and understand your feelings about it, and figure out ways to rebuild your life. This personal journal can be a comforting and illuminating companion in your recovery from job loss. Writing in a journal gives you a way to collect your thoughts, provides you with a tool to reflect upon and interpret your feelings, and gives you a place to record your memories, experiences, and ideas.

Studies on job loss support the idea that expressing thoughts and feelings in writing helps in dealing with the emotional and practical issues. Even people who don't necessarily share their feelings and thoughts with others can benefit from the process of keeping a journal. Some people prefer to write only about the practical side of job loss and the return to the workplace, and this is certainly helpful. But research also suggests that people who focus their writing on their emotional experiences, as well as practical matters, are likely to better cope with and work through job loss and unemployment. Writing about your thoughts and feelings may seem peripheral, but data have shown that dealing with emotional issues is central to recovering from job loss and rebuilding your life.

Sharing Your Experiences and Getting Help

Although people handle problems differently, many still share the same experiences. For example, peers who have been laid off with you may handle their situation in a particular manner, but they can understand and share similar experiences. Many people have lost their jobs, but many people have also successfully overcome the accompanying difficulties and challenges of job loss. Take heart then in knowing that with the right sort of perspective and support you too can emerge from this difficult time, perhaps more powerful and capable than when you started.

People who focus their writing on their emotional experiences, as well as practical matters, are likely to better cope with and work through job loss and unemployment.

Dealing with any kind of loss can be difficult. People who lose a job often experience a loss of identity, direction, pride, self-esteem, confidence, and trust, as well as security. At a time like this, the reflective work that is part of emotional recovery can be especially difficult, and exploring these thoughts and feelings in writing may make you feel uncomfortable, vulnerable, or put you in touch with emotions you'd rather avoid.

Seek help whenever you find yourself feeling especially pained, vulnerable, or lost. A support network—family, friends, neighbors, members of your church or temple, or others in your community—is important during any period of recovery, but even this might not be enough. If you find the accompanying feelings especially difficult to bear or the issues overwhelming and confusing, seek help from a trained counselor, therapist, clergy member, social worker, or psychiatrist.

Moving Through *The Healing Journey Through Job Loss*

Reading and using *The Healing Journey Through Job Loss* is a positive step along this uninvited, but nonetheless present, road in your life. Using this book is one key to surviving job loss, healing emotional wounds, planning ahead, and moving on.

If you're working with a counselor, she or he may assign a specific chapter or journal entry for you. If you're working on your own, where should you start? *The Healing Journey Through Job Loss* was designed to be used in the sequence presented, and the progression of chapters and journal entries is built upon the stages of job loss recovery and self-renewal described in Chapter 2. However, it will be important to consider which of your needs and problems is most pressing. The next chapter ("A Road Map Through Job Loss") will help you assess where you are in your recovery from job loss and help you pick the best place to start your healing journey.

In general, it's a good idea to glance through *The Healing Journey Through Job Loss* so you're familiar with its format and ideas, but don't rush through it. Just as you can't recover from the impact of job loss overnight, you shouldn't try—or expect—to complete your journal in a few days. Although there's no "right" pace for dealing with emotional issues, consider working through one chapter at a time, staying with it until you've completed all the relevant journal entries in that chapter. This will give you time to reread and think about what you've written before moving on to the next aspect of your reflective and recovery work.

Making Yourself Comfortable

You may or may not be used to keeping a diary or journal, and perhaps you feel unsure about how to start. Regardless of which chapter or entry you start with, you need to decide on the conditions and environment that will best support your journal writing. Here are a few suggestions that can help make the process more comfortable and productive for you:

- Set aside a regular schedule for working through your journal, preferably at a time of day when you're fresh and have the most energy.

- Take breaks during your writing if you need to. Stretching your legs can also give your mind a break.

- Consider playing some quiet music or other relaxing background sounds.

- Pick a place to read and write that will be physically comfortable for you.

- Pick a place to read and write that will be emotionally comfortable for you as well. Do you prefer a quiet, private location or a public area?

- Once you've completed an entry, reread it. Reflecting on what you've written can help you gain new insights.

Set aside a regular schedule for working through your journal, preferably at a time of day when you're fresh and have the most energy.

Using the Entries

The styles for different journal entries in *The Healing Journey Through Job Loss* are often different from one another, and each entry is provided only once. There are some entry formats that you may especially like using, and there are entries that you'll want to repeat more than once. Feel free to keep a supplemental journal in addition to this book where you can add your "spill-over" thoughts or additional entries. You may also want to photocopy certain blank entries so that you can complete them more than once.

Each journal entry is completed by "Things to Think About," a series of questions for you to consider after you've completed your entry. These are not a formal part of the entry but are reflective points that may spark a further journal entry, serve as discussion points if you're sharing your experience with a friend or counselor, or simply act as a focal point for your thoughts.

The Value of Your Journal

If you have a problem expressing your thoughts and feelings to others, writing can be cathartic, allowing you to unburden yourself in private.

Much of the benefit of *The Healing Journey Through Job Loss* comes from gaining skills in reflection and self-expression. As you answer questions or write your thoughts in a journal entry, you're having a "conversation" with yourself. Even if you have a problem expressing your thoughts and feelings to others, writing can be cathartic, allowing you to unburden yourself in private. The main thing is that you *are* expressing what you think and feel. Your journal can be of great value as you work through the issues surrounding your job loss.

Recovering and Rebuilding after Job Loss

The word *recovery* is used throughout *The Healing Journey Through Job Loss* to characterize your path back to work and emotional well-being. The same idea can be expressed in a number of different ways, each with a slightly different meaning.

- Recuperation, or returning to health or strength
- Revival, or coming back to life
- Rescue, or to set free or to save
- Reestablishment, or getting back into the game
- Restoration, or returning to former strength or glory
- Renewal, or rebirth

Any of these meanings are apt descriptions of the process you face. The goal is to move beyond recovery to rebuilding and renewal.

Recovery is also intended to describe your ability to work through this challenging time without becoming overcome by circumstances, swept away by your emotions, or feeling defeated. Recovery *doesn't* mean a return to the ways things were before. It *does* mean coming through intact and solvent.

Job Loss and Your Family

Many people in the workforce have families, and their families are affected as much, or almost as much, by job loss as they are themselves. In fact, if you have a family, your concern for them may be a significant source of additional stress and worry. Throughout *The Healing Journey Through Job Loss,* you'll be urged to discuss your situation with important family members, seek their opinions, make plans and significant decisions with them, and turn to them for support and inspiration. This is *your* journal, not your family's, but *your* job loss is probably *their* job loss too. Consider involving your family as much as possible at every step of your journey.

Recovery doesn't mean a return to the ways things were before. It does mean coming through intact and solvent.

2

A Road Map Through Job Loss

EVE

Of course, I knew about layoffs. How can you work in modern society and not hear about the thousands that get laid off each month? One merger between big companies, and thousands can get fired at one time. Still, it was always something that only happened to other people and in other firms. Even after we got new management, we were assured that no one would lose their jobs. Of course, that was a load of hogwash.

Just two weeks before I was laid off, I was promised that my job in management was vital to the company. When my boss came up to me and told me that I no longer had a job, I was flabbergasted. I had to leave at the end of that workday! No notice, just a thank-you letter, a final check that included accrued vacation, sick time, and a severance allowance, and insurance forms to complete asking if I wanted to continue to subscribe at my own cost.

I still haven't recovered. I'm looking daily for a job now, but how can anything take the place of sixteen years of climbing the ladder and investment in one job? It's not just like losing a paycheck. It's more like losing a way of life. I feel cheated and used. I feel angry.

I feel worried. I don't really know what's ahead for me now or the best way to proceed.

HOW PEOPLE RESPOND to the loss of a job will vary greatly. Clearly, some people are able to shrug their shoulders and walk away from the event. Others will find it devastating. The response of different individuals will likely be tied to many variables: their approach to life, their investment in a particular job or career, their age, or their financial or family responsibilities, and so on.

For many people, however, there's no question that job loss is a "loss" in the broadest sense of the word. A loss can be described simply: you had something and now it's gone. When the loss is important, however, attached to that *physical* loss is a complex web of *feelings*. When you've invested something of yourself in the thing that's now lost, grief and despair usually follow. It's probably accurate to say that people who are *not* deeply affected by job loss didn't have a high level of personal investment in that particular job. For them, the job was more a secondary feature of their lives, rather than a primary foundation upon which much of their life was built. This is not true for many employees in the workplace who deeply count upon their jobs to provide income, security, stability, consistency, direction, relationships, and identity. These people are most likely going to experience their job loss as a personal "loss," not just as a loss of income or as a necessary change in life.

Whether we like it or not, work is a defining feature of our daily lives and implicit in our identity in society. The novelist William Faulkner remarked that "one of the saddest things is that the only thing (you) can do for eight hours a day, day after day, is work. You can't eat eight hours a day nor drink for eight hours a day nor make love for eight hours."

The Impact of Job Loss

Although it's true that some people are able to take a job loss in stride and adapt quickly, it's equally true that job loss can have a far-ranging impact on people's lives. The impact of job loss will be tied to your personality style, your previous experiences, and your investment in and dependence upon your job. There are at least two primary aspects to job loss: the *practical* reality of losing your job and the *emotional* reality. In the first case, losing a job means loss of primary income and all the financial consequences attached to that reality. Job loss can eat through savings, require bank or personal loans, force relocation, require retraining for another profession, leave you without health insurance, and affect your lifestyle in general. These represent some of the obvious and tangible consequences from job loss. But for most, there are equally real emotional consequences of job loss, which can also be quite tangible: changes in self-image and personal identity, feelings that well up as you think about your job and your former employer, fears about your future and your ability to recover from this massive change in your life, and perhaps concerns about how you may be seen by others now that you've lost your job.

A third aspect of job loss involves *structural* changes in your daily life. How do you use your time now that you no longer have a job to attend each day or work that you bring home each evening? If you have a family, how do you interact with your spouse and children in a life and set of relationships that may once have been dominated by your work?

Most of the material that you're likely to read will touch upon the need to get back on the horse and refrain from sitting back feeling sorry for yourself. These books and articles will instruct you to think ahead, design a plan for yourself, and get back into

The impact of job loss will be tied to your personality style, your previous experiences, and your investment in and dependence upon your job.

Seeking and finding a job without recognizing, understanding, and addressing emotional consequences may undermine your ability to recover fully from job loss, both in terms of the job you wind up with and your attitude about yourself and your work.

the action. They'll direct you to not fall into despair and self-pity or anger and resentment. Many of your friends and family members will also urge you to find a way to move on and not get stuck. Although it may never be stated quite this clearly, you'll be directed to "get over it" and be offered ideas and words of wisdom and encouragement: "It's all for the best," "This is the way it was meant to be," "You'll find something better," and so on. In fact, these are all quite appropriate and supportive responses, all intended with your best interests at heart. Nevertheless, all the support and pep talks in the world can't necessarily overcome the very real and deep impact of job loss. There are other consequences to consider when you lose a job, and it may take you longer to heal despite the supportive and encouraging actions of your friends and family.

Seeking and finding a job without recognizing, understanding, and addressing emotional consequences may undermine your ability to recover fully from job loss, both in terms of the job you wind up with *and* your attitude about yourself and your work. It will be important for you to not feel that there's something wrong with you just because you can't follow the advice of family, friends, and books and simply move on without emotional baggage weighing you down.

The Work of Recovery and Rebuilding

For some, job loss led to a situation from which they were never able to recover or fully reconstitute their lives. For others, job loss proved a boon, an uninvited event that forced upon them unexpected opportunities for personal and professional growth and the chance to change and improve their lives significantly. In fact, it's not unusual to hear of people who look back at their job loss with gratitude because the situation forced them onto new roads that they would never have otherwise discovered or taken.

Chances are that *you* will find a new job. It may not be your first choice, and you may even have to take on work you dislike or feel is below or outside of your skill level. One way or another, the practical aspects of job loss are likely to get resolved, at least to some degree. Most people who lose their jobs do find another one. But this doesn't necessarily add up to a satisfactory situation, either financially or emotionally, and the emotional issues may not be resolved.

Unaddressed or unresolved emotional issues may significantly affect the way in which you see and experience yourself. In turn, this will directly influence the way you approach finding a new job, what you will accept as your new conditions of employment, and how you settle into your new job or changed lifestyle. In the end, "recovery" is both economic *and* emotional. It involves both finding a new job or source of income that meets your financial needs *and* resolving the personal issues raised by losing your job in the first place.

Four Stages of Recovery and Rebuilding

Shakespeare wrote in *The Merchant of Venice,* "You take my life when you do take the means whereby I live." These words might exemplify your feelings and fears as you realize you've lost your job. As you face, deal with, and recover from this sudden shift in the direction your life has taken, you'll pass through several stages. Each stage has several primary tasks associated with it— successfully working your way through each of these tasks prepares you for the work in the following stage. In addition to these tasks, every stage has an overarching goal as you work your way through it.

Viewing the process of recovery and rebuilding as a connected sequence of stages is useful. It helps you make sense of your experiences as you move from the coping with job loss stage to the

"You take my life when you do take the means whereby I live."
—SHAKESPEARE,
The Merchant of Venice

self-renewal stage. Understanding this process as an experience that develops and changes over time can help you maintain your composure even when you may feel anxious and insecure. Recognizing that each stage has a goal and set of tasks provides you with a language to understand and describe your experience and a map to help pinpoint your location along this journey.

As you think about each stage described below, consider how the stages overlap. Stages aren't concrete things that have a definite beginning and a clear end point but are phases that seamlessly grow from and blend into one another.

STAGE 1: COPING

People who lose their jobs due to staff cutbacks, reorganization, business relocations, or closings often lose their job without much warning, or any warning at all. When a job loss is completely unexpected, or at least unexpected at that time or on that day, Stage 1 is likely to involve shock and disbelief. In this case, the precursor to recovery is a sense of disorientation as your world suddenly crumbles. As disorientation wears off and reality begins to take hold, it's not unusual for disillusionment or anger to quickly follow.

For those who knew that job loss was coming, either because they strongly suspected such an eventuality or were directly informed, this first stage begins not with disorientation, which may be fleeting at best, but with disillusionment. Their belief that they had security and safety in a job, or that they had value to their company, is shattered.

This stage begins with a sense of disorientation and ends as you grapple and cope with the disillusionment that often follows.

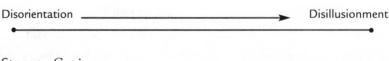

Stage 1: Coping

The broad goal of this stage is to survive this initial period without doing anything destructive to yourself, your future options, or your relationships. The life tasks of Stage 1 include:

1. *Adjusting to this new reality*. Although you may not accept the fairness, necessity of your job loss, or the reasons behind it, you must nevertheless be able to accept its reality and adjust to the changes it's brought to your life.

2. *Handling immediate responses*. This task involves your ability to appropriately handle your initial emotional responses. People can do some wild things after suddenly, and perhaps unfairly, losing their job.

3. *Dealing with issues of self-esteem and humiliation*. No matter how well you may rationalize it, job loss has a way of eating away at self-image. This task involves valuing yourself and dealing with this situation without letting shame or embarrassment stand in your way.

4. *Coping with family issues*. If you have a spouse, children, or others who depend on your strength as well as your income, this task means facing their fears as well as your own and involving them fully in your journey—because it's their journey also.

"Sure I am of this, that you have only to endure to conquer. You have only to persevere to save yourselves."
—WINSTON CHURCHILL

STAGE 2: SURVIVING

As you enter the second stage of your recovery, disillusionment begins to fade into the past. It's not that you feel any less disillusioned or bitter, but you've learned to cope with these particular feelings and are ready to move on without getting pulled under by them. You begin to deal with issues of survival and the restoration of emotional and financial stability. This stage involves laying the foundation upon which you'll begin to rebuild your life and includes emotional, practical, and financial tasks as you consider how you can survive this blow. As you near and enter this stage, your focus is on basic survival—getting through this enormously difficult time in your life.

Survival   ———————————————→   Stabilization

Stage 2: Surviving

In this stage, the general goal is to create a base of comfort and safety upon which you can build your new life. The tasks include:

1. *Stabilizing your immediate life.* Here, you're dealing with putting the brakes on a life that may be running out of control—loss of income, a different daily schedule, and emotions that may be running high. The task is to find a way to manage the events of your daily life so that things start to once again resemble normalcy.

2. *Building support.* Support comes in all forms from the love and concern of family and friends to concrete assistance in getting a new job or source of income. This task involves learning to recognize, use, and build a support network.

3. *Managing your emotions and behaviors.* Even though exercising control over immediate emotional responses and behavioral reactions is a primary task of Stage 1, you're going to feel strong emotions for days, weeks, and even years after losing your job. The task is learning to recognize feelings and manage accompanying behaviors that may be self-destructive or destructive to others, self-defeating, or inappropriate.

4. *Maintaining perspective.* From fears of lost income and prestige to a sense of never being able to fully recover what is now lost, job loss can clearly be overwhelming. The task is keeping a clear head and not falling into a pattern of distorted or negative thinking about your past, present, or future.

Support comes in all forms from the love and concern of family and friends to concrete assistance in getting a new job or source of income.

STAGE 3: ASSESSMENT AND PLANNING

With your life more stable and on an even keel, the emotional and practical tasks of this stage involve a frank evaluation of your life situation with a focus on where to go from here. The movement is from assessment and self-valuation as you enter the stage to a point where you feel that you have regained control of your life.

"You can see a lot just by looking."
——YOGI BERRA

Assessment ————————————▶ Regained Control

Stage 3: Assessment and Planning

The primary goal of this stage is the assessment of your needs, skills, and dreams, as well as the needs and dreams of family members who are accompanying you on this journey. Primary tasks include:

1. *Taking stock of your life*. This task involves an evaluation and inventory of your skills, assets, interests, and resources. It provides the basis for meaningful movement and change as you move on with recovery and self-renewal.

2. *Assessing your choices*. This task is part of a trio that involves inventorying, evaluating, and planning. Here the goals are considering decisions you have available to you and developing a basis for making choices.

3. *Developing plans*. Connected to other tasks in this early stage, the task is to focus on how to put your ideas into action and implement change.

4. *Rebuilding self-image*. As you work through the tasks of Stage 3, an overarching goal is that of feeling good about yourself and confident in your skills, choices, and ability to move on.

STAGE 4: DECISION MAKING AND SELF-RENEWAL

The work of prior stages represented a time-out from life—an opportunity to pull yourself together, reconnect with family and friends, and reflect. The work of this stage represents the end of this journey—your recovery from this loss and your moving on to your life ahead. The overarching goal for this final stage in your journey is that of self-determination. It involves the active implementation of your plans as you move in the direction that you and, where appropriate, your family have chosen.

Decision Making ⟶ Self-Renewal

Stage 4: Decision Making and Self-Renewal

As you move from decision making to self-renewal, the tasks of this stage include:

1. *Implementing decisions.* Beyond thinking about and making decisions, in this final stage your task is to put your plans into action, to turn ideas and decisions into reality.

2. *Accepting personal responsibility.* It's not always possible, or desirable, *to* accept personal responsibility for the things that happen to you. Many times, these things are simply outside of your control. But, in this final stage of your recovery, it will be important to recognize and accept that you are responsible for all of your *choices* and *behaviors*, both successful and unsuccessful.

3. *Taking emotional risks.* An old English proverb says "a smooth sea never made a skillful mariner." This characterizes much of the struggle you'll face at every stage of your recovery and rebuilding and in every task. The proverb aptly summarizes the need to take risks that are, perhaps, more emo-

"Life breaks everyone, and afterwards many are stronger at the broken places."
—ERNEST HEMINGWAY

tional than anything else: the risk of disappointment, the risk of failure, the risk of change.

4. *Regaining self-confidence.* The end point of your journey is the renewal, and perhaps enrichment, of your self-confidence. This task, perhaps more than all the others, represents the sum total of all your travels and all your successes.

The Journey

There's no "right" pace for this journey, no "correct" length of time spent in each stage. Some people may spend only several days at any given stage, quickly moving on to the next stage. Others will have a more difficult time moving from one stage to another. Sheer willpower and tenacity alone won't get you from one end of your journey to the other. Rebuilding after job loss, like recovery from any other form of loss, is a process that takes place over time. Your personality, your approach, your resilience, and your support system are just a few factors that will influence the time you will need to recover and renew yourself.

The important thing to note about stages is that not fully completing tasks in one stage can hinder a person from achieving the tasks in the next stage. Although one can work on the tasks of any given stage of recovery without being fully prepared, it is likely one will not accomplish as much. It's equally true that people can get emotionally "stuck" in one stage and fail to move on at all.

So how long should someone be at any given stage? There's no answer. This is a question you have to pursue for yourself to find your own answers. If you do decide you're stuck, then it's time to reach out and get some more help. We can't always do it all by ourselves.

You may already have a clear sense of what tasks need to be

The end point of your journey is the renewal, and perhaps enrichment, of your self-confidence.

completed first as you get back into the game. On the other hand, you may be so frazzled and overcome by feelings and worry that nothing's really clear. Either way, the journal entries in this chapter will help you pinpoint where to begin and what tasks are most pertinent at this point.

CHECKPOINT: STAGES

Based upon the descriptions in the preceding pages, circle the letter that most closely describes where you are *right now* with each task.

Stage 1 Tasks	I'm not ready to deal with this task.	I'm working on this task.	I've completed this task.
Adjusting to this new reality	A	B	C
Handling immediate responses	A	B	C
Dealing with self-esteem and humiliation	A	B	C
Coping with family issues	A	B	C
Stage 2 Tasks			
Stabilizing your immediate life	A	B	C
Building support	A	B	C
Managing your emotions and behaviors	A	B	C
Maintaining perspective	A	B	C
Stage 3 Tasks			
Taking stock of your life	A	B	C
Assessing your choices	A	B	C
Developing plans	A	B	C
Rebuilding self-image	A	B	C

Stage 4 Tasks	I'm not ready to deal with this task.	I'm working on this task.	I've completed this task.
Implementing decisions	A	B	C
Accepting personal responsibility	A	B	C
Taking emotional risks	A	B	C
Regaining self-confidence	A	B	C

Getting Located

You're now aware of the stages involved in job recovery and how they typically progress, and your Checkpoint entry has helped you identify where you are with respect to each of the tasks. Let's review the Checkpoint answers you've circled.

WHERE ARE YOU?

1. Which four tasks are most relevant to you *now*, in your current stage?

a. _____

b. _____

c. _____

d. _____

2. What do the tasks you picked tell you about the steps immediately ahead in the work of recovery and rebuilding?

_____

_____

3. What's your current stage in dealing with job loss? (If it's difficult for you to easily identify your current stage, go directly to the next step in this entry.)

_____

_____

4. Was it difficult for you to easily identify your current stage? If so, why?

_____

_____

_____

_____

THINGS TO THINK ABOUT

- Does the idea that there are "stages" to recovering and rebuilding after job loss fit your own experience?
- If you have a spouse or children, how are their needs and concerns affecting you and your decision-making process? Have you been sharing with them enough about what's going on for you?

Using Your Feelings as a Guide

You now have a sense of your current stage, but there's no quick way to work through the emotional issues and life situations created by your job loss. If recovering from job loss simply meant finding a new job, you wouldn't be using this journal. Instead, you'd be reading the classifieds. But for many people who lose their jobs, recovery and rebuilding are matters that involve emotions as well as finding new work. Job loss, for many displaced workers, is not a simple inconvenience, but an event that triggers a substantial life crisis.

Job loss is not a simple inconvenience, but an event that triggers a substantial life crisis.

Rebuilding life after a job loss doesn't just mean getting a new job; it also means doing the reflective work that underpins self-renewal. This sort of healing isn't simply the result of plowing through each day or even finding a new job. It's the sort of healing that's very much connected to understanding what has happened, and then using your insights as a source for personal understanding, creativity, decision making, and movement.

Thinking about what you've lost is an important component of any reflective work. But the key to healing is allowing yourself to *experience* the mass of feelings that has followed your job loss, and then sorting through and expressing them. Emotions are a critical part of being human. Unfortunately, people can respond to emotions and let their behaviors be guided by them inappropriately. This can sometimes lead to problems that contribute to difficult emotional experiences. The goal of reflective work is not to find ways to avoid, ignore, or bypass difficult and unpleasant feelings. Instead, the purpose is to find ways to recognize and accept difficult feelings and to learn to tolerate, manage, and work through them.

Feelings, even bad ones, can serve as a guide, helping you to make sense of what's going on inside. If you get in touch with your feelings, not just try to squelch or get rid of the negative ones, they can help point to the issues that are affecting you and provide direction in how to best deal with these triggers. Unfortunately, some people can't recognize their own feelings or are only able to recognize their most familiar emotions.

When people experience the same emotions over and over, for instance, they may be able to recognize one particular feeling and may even have become comfortable with this familiar feeling —even if it's an unpleasant emotion like anger or depression. Because the feeling has become familiar, they may fail to notice the web of other emotions that are often layered beneath and contributing to that feeling. In fact, it's easy to get stuck in one emotional state. But, in order to understand and manage intense emotions, you need to recognize, experience, and express *each* feeling. As you work through them, the intensity of each feeling will eventually fade to the point where you can function and move on.

The next journal entry lists many of the emotions commonly associated with loss and major life change. This checklist can help

The key to healing is allowing yourself to experience the mass of feelings that has followed your job loss, and then sorting through and expressing them.

you sort out your feelings and select the chapter in *The Healing Journey Through Job Loss* that will help you process your most intense emotions at the moment.

IDENTIFYING YOUR FEELINGS

Check all of the emotions that best describe what you are generally experiencing at this point in your life. (The numbers in parentheses next to each feeling indicate the chapters most relevant to dealing with that feeling or issue.)

___anger

Anger often feels like a physical thing. Your muscles tense up, and you may feel like yelling at someone or hitting something. Your rage may be aimed at your former employer, or you may find yourself getting angry at other people, society, or even yourself.

(7, 14)

___anxiety

Anxiety is distinct from fear and is often a generalized feeling. If you're afraid, at least you know what scares you. If you're anxious, on the other hand, you're likely to feel agitated without knowing exactly why. You may experience cold sweats, hyperactivity, or edginess.

(7, 8, 14)

___bitterness

Life may feel very unjust, and you may feel cheated and disappointed. You may feel victimized by your former employer, and you may feel jealous and resentful toward others who still have their jobs.

(4, 5, 10)

___concern about a plan for the future

You're worried about planning for your own future, but have little sense of how to develop a plan.

(8, 11, 12, 15)

__concern about relationships	You're not sure how your job loss will affect the way people see you, or how your relationships will be affected.	(5, 6, 10)
__concern about your family	You're not sure how your family will deal with your job loss, how to involve family, or if you want to involve them at all.	(3, 4, 5, 6)
__depression	Depression can be a general mood of melancholy or a full-blown experience that is all-encompassing and seems to have no end. In a major depression, your mood, appetite, sleep, memory, and ability to concentrate are seriously impaired. You may feel the impulse to do self-destructive things in an effort to find relief.	(4, 7, 14)
__fear	You're scared of what life will be like now. You may be fearful about finding another job, making enough money, having to make major lifestyle changes, or other practical concerns, or about your ability to cope emotionally.	(4, 7)
__feeling overwhelmed	You simply can't cope with the barrage of emotions, thoughts, and changes facing you. You feel like running away or escaping by using alcohol or drugs. You want someone to come and rescue you and to make it all go away.	(4, 6, 7, 8, 14)
__guilt	You may feel that you're responsible for your job loss or the position you or your family are now in. You may feel you should have worked harder, or you should have seen this coming and acted to avert the situation.	(4, 5, 7, 10)

__helplessness	Things seem outside of your control. You may be feeling as though you are on a roller-coaster ride and can't get off, or that you can't cope with the practicalities of your everyday life and feel unable to control or manage your feelings.	(3, 4, 6, 8, 11)
__inadequacy	You're feeling as though your job loss is the result of your personal failure—if you were more competent this would never have happened. You feel as though you're not good enough.	(4, 5, 6, 13)
__incompleteness	Without your work you feel empty and unable to function as a productive individual, incapable of fulfilling your needs in other ways.	(4, 5, 9, 13)
__preoccupation	You can't stop thinking about your job loss. Perhaps you keep replaying certain scenes over and over in your mind, or repeatedly get angry with your former employer. It's difficult to concentrate on your everyday responsibilities or engage in a conversation without your mind drifting back to the job.	(3, 4, 7, 10, 13)
__shame	You may feel that your job loss is a reflection on you and experience a sense of personal failure or fear that others will see it that way. Shame has a great deal to do with your sense of self-esteem, but even people with the highest self-regard can feel ashamed when it comes to losing their job.	(4, 5, 6, 7)
__shock	You're bewildered and still can't believe what's happened. You're hoping to wake up from a bad dream.	(3, 4, 7, 8)

Of the feelings you checked off, which three are most intense right now?

1. _____

_____

2. _____

_____

3. _____

_____

THINGS TO THINK ABOUT

- Do you share your feelings with anyone else? If not, what stops you?
- Do your feelings seem so intense at times that you can't handle them? If so, have you ever considered seeking professional help?

Beginning Your Journey

The background information provided so far is intended to help you place your experience in its *emotional* context. Most likely, you're experiencing the *normal* emotions and thoughts that follow job loss. Armed with that knowledge, it's now time for you to begin your reflective journey, dealing with both the emotional and practical aspects of your recovery from that loss.

The previous journal entry provided a way for you to think about those issues that are most pressing right now. If you want to work on any one of these feelings, or the issues connected to those feelings, immediately turn to the chapters whose numbers are given in the parentheses to the right of each feeling on the list on pages 24–26. If you want to work through *The Healing Journey Through Job Loss* sequentially, you may still want to come back to this list every now and then to see which feelings are most pressing at any given time.

CHECKING IN WITH YOURSELF

Complete these five sentences.

1. *As I complete this chapter, I feel like . . .* _____

_____

_____

2. *Right now, I'd like to . . .* _____

_____

_____

3. *Lately, I've been feeling like . . .* _____

_____

_____

4. *My most important current task is . . .* _____

_____

_____

5. *I feel like I most need to work on . . .* _____

_____

_____

THINGS TO THINK ABOUT

- Do you have a clear sense of the sort of issues, feelings, and tasks that you'll be facing in your recovery work?
- Will you work your way through *The Healing Journey Through Job Loss* in the sequence provided, or will you move through the book in your own order?
- Are the problems you're experiencing so severe or debilitating that you need support and help from a friend or assistance from a professional counselor?
- If you have family members who are clearly affected by your job loss and have a big stake in your life, are you checking with them about their feelings and concerns? Are you asking them for their opinions, ideas, and support as you make decisions about your joint lives?

3

Destination:

DEALING WITH REALITY

"Obviously there's a lot more in play here than the simple question of finding a job."

—G. J. MEYER

ALLEN

I knew things weren't working out with my new job. Although I didn't want to believe it, I had this sinking feeling that I was going to be fired. Sure enough I was right. They said things just weren't "working out" the way they'd expected. But although I was half expecting that news, I really was taken aback when I heard the words. As soon as I got back into the privacy of my own office, I found my eyes welling up with tears, and my emotions clogged up with fear, anger, and humiliation. I had no idea how I was going to tell anyone else in my office what had just happened, let alone my family and friends.

I'd given up a lot to take this new job. I'd quit my old job and closed my small consulting practice, and we'd put our house up for sale and leased a house closer to this new job. This wasn't just a new job; this was a new life. And now there was no old life to go back to. When I took the job, I just never imagined anything like this could happen.

I wondered if the people who hired and fired me had any idea, or even cared, about the effects of their decision on my life and the life

29

of my family. I suppose it didn't really matter. All that counted was that I was left high and dry and had to figure out how to deal with all this chaos.

SOME PEOPLE KNOW job loss is coming. Others suspect it, but hope they're wrong. Some plan ahead, but the ax comes before they can leave under their own steam and on their own terms. Still others are completely unsuspecting, taken quite off balance by the news that they've been fired.

When the day came for you, whether you were surprised or not, you may have been quite shocked. Being *surprised* in this case means being newly introduced to the idea that you've lost your job. Being *shocked* means that you were deeply affected emotionally when you actually heard the news, even if you were expecting to be fired.

On the other hand, perhaps you accepted dismissal casually, whether you expected it or not. Quite possibly, you expected to step into another position of equal rank or status easily, only to wake up to the reality that this other job just isn't there for you. It may have taken some time—and much frustration, disappointment, and fear—for this new awareness to dawn on you.

The loss of your job has been followed not only by unemployment, but an assault on your emotions and a sense of helplessness and frustration as you wait for something better to happen.

Most likely, you're one of thousands of people who've lost their jobs without the practical or emotional resources and plans required for a smooth transition between jobs or sources of income. The loss of your job has been followed not only by unemployment, but an assault on your emotions and a sense of helplessness and frustration as you wait for something better to happen.

Of course, there are plenty of people who quickly replace one job with another. But your experience of job loss is not simply about losing a job. It involves your introduction (and in some cases your reintroduction, if this isn't your first experience with job loss) to a demoralizing and often frightening slice of the world. For you, the issue isn't simply about *finding* a job. It involves the *reclamation* of a job and the status and identity embodied by that position. It involves the reconstruction of your life and the renewal of your identity. But first, it involves coming to terms and being able to deal with this reality.

Processing Your Relationship

In society, people and work are intimately connected. People are defined by their jobs, and often gear their lives around their work, rather than the other way around. A relationship exists between you and your job. It may be purely financial, or it may serve as a source of personal satisfaction and an outlet for your creativity. It may be a love-hate relationship or the basis upon which you build other important nonwork aspects of your life. When that relationship ends, emotional upheaval can follow, *especially* if you weren't the one who ended it.

According to Freud, the ability to work and the ability to love are two of our most critical needs. In many ways, being laid off is like being left by a lover. The emotional responses are often as strong or stronger. Just as some people deny that the loss of a love relationship has upset them, some people will deny that their loss of a job has affected them emotionally. Dealing with reality means acknowledging your feelings and thoughts and working through them.

Processing your feelings and experiences may not immediately help you to feel better, but it's one step along an important path. As you process your experiences, you begin to better understand what you're going through "below the surface," on a gut level, and you are able to understand the emotional forces within you that might otherwise be invisible to you. It's that internal emotional experience that people often refer to as "excess baggage,"

People and work are intimately connected. People are defined by their jobs, and often gear their lives around their work, rather than the other way around.

and it's that baggage that can affect your ability to make good decisions and undermine your future relationships.

Processing can not only lead to increased self-awareness, it can also allow you the opportunity to transform "raw" emotional experiences into a more refined product that can help you cope with your job loss and move on with your life.

WITHOUT MY JOB

Complete each sentence that follows.

1. *My relationship with my job can best be described as* . . . _____
_____
_____

2. *When I think of this relationship, I* . . . _____
_____
_____

3. *The most difficult part of this relationship was* . . . _____
_____
_____

4. *My greatest regret about this relationship is* . . . _____
_____
_____

5. Pick five words to describe your feelings about getting fired, and explain each.

       I feel . . .   *because* . . .

a. _____   _____
b. _____   _____
c. _____   _____
d. _____   _____
e. _____   _____

6. *Without my job, I'm . . .* _____

_____

_____

_____

7. What have you learned about yourself from this relationship?

_____

_____

_____

_____

_____

8. As you complete this entry, answer these questions.

a. *Right now, I feel . . .* _____

_____

b. *Right now, I think . . .* _____

_____

THINGS TO THINK ABOUT

- Is it difficult for you to think of yourself as getting fired? Do you prefer to describe your job loss in a different way? If it is difficult or awkward, why?
- In Question 5, you described your *feelings* in the left-hand column and your *thoughts* in the right-hand column. Can you usually tell the difference between thinking and feeling?

The Stress of Job Loss

What makes it possible for one person to lose a job and move on without fuss, while others simply can't find a job or escape the effects of unemployment? Losing a job doesn't *necessarily* result in demoralization, panic, or insecurity. Neither does it automatically mean remaining unemployed. Many unemployed people take jobs outside of their field or speciality, accept lower pay or rank, or take temporary jobs. Actors and writers, for instance, do this quite routinely as a stopgap measure. Because their ultimate goal is to make a living in their profession, their identities and integrity aren't threatened by work outside of their real interests. Outside work becomes a necessary part of earning money between gigs. Of course, artists who can *never* find work in their field begin to feel just as challenged and fearful as lawyers, teachers, factory workers, and CEOs who lose their jobs. This clearly points to the underlying issue: the turmoil brought by job loss has less to do with the loss of a job itself than with the loss of what the job *represents*.

The turmoil brought by job loss has less to do with the loss of a job itself than with the loss of what the job represents.

Income, financial security, stability and consistency, personal expectations, career goals, status and the respect of the community, and self-esteem are just a few of the things that work represents. Some of these are *concrete* realities, grounded in the ability to securely support ourselves and our families and live comfortably. Other factors are less tangible. They're more connected to the *idea* that work itself is essential and to a fear that unemployment strips us of our worth in the eyes of others. As exemplified by the words of the Spanish statesman and philosopher José Ortega y Gasset, without work many of us feel empty: "An 'unemployed' existence is a worse negation of life than death itself." In short, most of us have a great deal invested in our work.

The stress caused by job loss depends on a number of factors. One is the availability of work. If there's no work to be had, then job loss is devastating. Under these circumstances, finding the "right" job becomes almost impossible. People may be required to take any job, regardless of the pay, conditions, nature of the work, or the emotional toll. It may even lead to pulling up roots, breaking ties, and moving to where the jobs are.

Other barriers are the lifestyle you hold and your personal expectations for work. For many people who are suddenly unemployed, accepting a transitory job is unacceptable, even unthinkable. The idea of lesser pay and rank or work in a different field, even on a temporary basis, is demeaning and frightening. It may feel like a concession to the idea that there is no way "back," and somehow the fall from grace is permanent.

The more meaning you attach to a certain type of job, salary range, health insurance and other benefits, long-term prospects, and pension plans, the more you invest in your work. The more your sense of personal worth, self-esteem, direction, and motivation are connected to your job, the greater the association between your identity and the job. These are the things that give your job meaning—what your job does for *you*. The more meaning you invest in your job, for whatever reason, the greater the stress is likely to be when the job fails you.

The more meaning you attach to a certain type of job, salary range, health insurance and other benefits, long-term prospects, and pension plans, the more you invest in your work.

WORK HAD MEANING BECAUSE . . .

1. *This job had meaning for me because it provided . . .*

___a steady income and practical benefits.

___opportunities for professional growth and career development.

___emotional security and stability.

___a sense of personal value and identity.

___a means for me to feel good about myself.

___a way to be seen by others as important and valuable.

___a means to live out my professional and personal interests.

___a sense of direction and purpose.

___job security and allowed me to develop retirement plans.

___supportive and important on-the-job relationships with coworkers.

__ a sense of belonging to a community.

__ a sense that I was doing something important.

__ a way to take care of my family.

__ something I could count on for my future.

__ a way to contribute to society.

__ a means for living out my dreams and ideals.

other: _____

_____

_____

_____

2. Which three factors were most important to you?

a. _____

b. _____

c. _____

3. Think about the factors and needs you identified. The job was primarily important because it fulfilled . . .

__ financial and practical needs.

__ professional and career needs.

__ emotional and personal needs.

other needs: _____

_____

4. *This job had meaning for me because . . .* _____

_____

5. *Without this job, I . . .* _____

_____

6. *Job loss has left me feeling . . .* _____

_____

Investments and Returns

Now you've lost your job, your investment, time, efforts, ideas, loyalty, and perhaps your hopes may seem all in vain. You may feel used, cheated, robbed, exploited, or victimized.

No doubt you expected some very concrete returns from your investment: a secure pension, a step up the career ladder, or the simple stability and comfort of a job that you could count on. But is the *only* return from your investment the job itself and its benefits? Are there other returns that you haven't noticed? Is it completely true that your whole investment vanished when you were laid off?

At this time you may *not* be able to notice other gains given how frazzled and upset you may be. It might be very difficult to think positively at a time like this when you're filled with feelings of all sorts—anger, bitterness, shock, fear, humiliation, sadness. Chances are the job loss has affected you on some emotional level. Looking for other sorts of returns on your investment after a stinging experience like this may feel silly. It may feel as though you're trying to look on the bright side when there *isn't* a bright side, but you're not! Instead, you're trying to understand this situation from more than one perspective, so you can draw as much as possible from it.

It's not that writing down your feelings or searching for meaning will necessarily make you feel better or make things magically disappear. The point of this process is to change *you*, so that

By reexamining a situation and reframing your experience, you learn to see more in it, not only about the situation but about yourself.

you can change your situation through your ideas, plans, and actions. It'll be important to make sure that you're not getting stuck in a reality dominated only by negative thoughts and emotions. If your interpretation of reality is skewed by powerful emotions, it may be distorted. This can lead to your missing things that are just off to the side, hidden perhaps from everyday life. By reexamining a situation and reframing your experience, you learn to see more in it, not only about the situation but about yourself. You learn to take from it what you can and use this a source for self-renewal.

In this next entry, begin by exploring what you put of yourself into the job and how your investment failed you. Then, start to think about ways that your investment *did* pay off. Perhaps your job served as a valuable training ground in a particular job or industry, or maybe it taught you something about how to behave or not behave in the world of work. Your resume is now fuller and richer than it was before this job, and you can take what you've learned to your new job. It could be that this loss has further fueled your determination to achieve professional goals in a competitive world or even made you decide that you're interested in a different profession. Just finding another perspective, no matter how tough, can represent a return on your investment if you can use what you've learned. There are *always* two sides to every story and always more than one sort of return on every investment.

RETURN ON YOUR INVESTMENT

1. In this job I invested my . . .

__beliefs	__best years	__commitment	__creativity
__dreams	__energy	__faith	__hopes
__ideas	__life	__loyalty	__money
__soul	__sweat	__time	__trust

other: _____   _____

_____   _____

_____   _____

2. In return for my investment, I hoped for . . .

__appreciation   __career development   __job security

__pension   __respect   __satisfaction

other: _____   _____

_____   _____

3. *I put in . . .* _____

_____

and in return I got . . . _____

_____

_____

4. *Now I feel . . .* _____

_____

_____

5. *I feel like I've lost . . .* _____

_____

_____

6. Complete the following sentence, checking all that apply and adding your own thoughts. *On the other side of things, I've gained . . .*

__a break from work   __a network of colleagues

__a pension   __business ideas

__career ideas   __direction and identity

__insights into the business   __insight into how to behave in the

    world   work world

__money in the bank

__new interests

__professional experience

__time to spend with my family

__valuable personal experience

__new friends

__new perspective

__wisdom

__training in my field/new skills

__the chance to do other things that
interest me

other: _____

_____

_____

_____

_____

_____

7. *Through this experience, I've learned about . . .*

__life   __my family   __my friends   __my profession

__myself   __new ideas   __other people   __the business world

__the world   __trust   __work   __what's important

other: _____

_____

_____

_____

_____

_____

8. What are the two most valuable returns on your investment, and why?

a. _____ because _____

b. _____ because _____

9. How can you make use of these returns in your recovery from job loss and move-ment toward self-renewal?

_____

_____

_____

_____

_____

Defining Reality

How you experience and define reality is up to you. Some people face awful times and curse their luck, and others say "praise be," prepared to believe that the events of their life are part of a larger scheme. When faced with adversity, some will see the situation as just one more of life's challenges to be overcome, and others will be ready to give up. Which is the "correct" reality when faced with the proverbial glass filled only to the midpoint, half-full or half-empty?

Right now, reality—your experience of daily life—is probably dominated and defined by your job loss. No doubt you think about and are affected by some aspect of that loss every day. One significant goal of *The Healing Journey Through Job Loss* is to provide you with a journal to help look into and explore many corners of your life, not just the obvious. Use your journal to record your everyday life, chronicle your experiences, and explore those side streets in your life. You'll find that there's more than one version of reality and more than one way to regain your footing and renew your life.

There are many ways to get from New York to San Francisco. No matter which way you go, your point of origin is always New York, and San Francisco is always your destination. It's the variety of routes you can take and the types of transportation

It's the variety of routes you can take and the types of transportation that define the journey. No one route is the correct one, nor is there just one means of travel.

that define the journey. No one route is the correct one, nor is there just one means of travel. Your journey has started with job loss, and your destination is self-renewal. The path you take will help define your reality.

NEW YORK TO SAN FRANCISCO

1. How many ways are there to get from New York to San Francisco? Name five means of transportation.

a. _____

b. _____

c. _____

d. _____

e. _____

2. Name five different routes to get from New York to San Francisco.

a. _____

b. _____

c. _____

d. _____

e. _____

3. How quickly can you get from New York to San Francisco?

_____

4. What's the slowest route you can imagine to get from New York to San Francisco?

_____

5. How long would it take you to get from New York to San Francisco if you took this slow route?

_____

6. Which is the best route to take? _____

_____

7. Why?

_____

_____

_____

8. Name those factors that might influence the route you take.

__adventure	__anxiety about trip	__companions on the trip
__costs of travel	__deadlines	__discovery
__fear of flying	__imagination	__novelty
__pleasure of the journey	__relaxation	__reluctance to slow down
__scenic route	__sight-seeing	__time limitations
__urgency of arrival	__variety	__visiting friends along the way

other: _____   _____

_____   _____

THINGS TO THINK ABOUT

- What's the relationship of this entry to your search for self-renewal?
- How can you decide which is the best route for you to take along your journey to self-renewal? What factors determine your reality?
- Who are your companions on this trip? How important is their input for planning this journey?

Letting Go

Letting go can be thought of as the ability to detach from and remain uninfluenced by the negative feelings often attached to difficult events and circumstances. It means dealing with stress unperturbed and undisturbed by events outside of your control. Letting go means being emotionally unaffected. When you let go, you drop your emotional baggage. Some people would call this "mellow." At the other extreme, rumination, anxiety, and worry contribute very little to problem solving and positive long-term outcomes.

It will be very difficult for you to let go of all the feelings—concern, worry, anxiety, fear, humiliation, and rejection you're probably experiencing—it would be great if you could just drop all the negative thoughts and feelings that are going around in your head. Unless you have a remarkable capacity for acceptance, relaxation, and coping, it's likely that you won't be able to let go of these feelings for quite some time.

Having said that, the ability to let go *is* an eventual goal. The goal is not necessarily to forget or even forgive, but to move on without the lead weight you may now feel. The goal is to be able to make healthy life choices without angrily looking back at this time in your life. Although chances are that letting go is not possible right now, it doesn't mean that you can't make a start even this early in your journey.

Here, letting go takes on a slightly different meaning. It's not the complete resolution of emotional issues and internal turmoil but the *unloading* of issues—sometimes referred to as *catharsis*. The first step to letting go is recognizing that you have something to let out in the first place. The second step to letting *go* is letting it *out*. For many, letting it out is no small task. Not everyone is comfortable with unleashing their thoughts and feelings. Some may attempt to extinguish, stifle, and get rid of their thoughts and feelings by growing numb, inappropriately using drugs or alcohol, under- or overeating, restricting their relationships with others, or engaging in other self-defeating or destructive behaviors that emotionally or physically harm them or others. One reason to keep a journal is that it allows you a place to let go and express yourself in a private way that's accessible only to you, unless you choose to share your journal with others.

Letting it out and letting go are parts of a process in which

The first step to letting go is recognizing that you have something to let out in the first place. The second step to letting go is letting it out.

people learn how to cope with and manage difficult feelings so that they can use these as a basis for emotional stability and personal growth. The next entry will provide a way to let things out. As with other entries, sentence starts are used to help jump-start your writing. But sentence starts can do more than push you in a particular direction. They can also serve as exercises in word association. One way to use a sentence start is to ponder the question and think hard before you complete the sentence. Another way is to let the idea just pop out by finishing the sentence in the first way that enters your mind, letting the sentence finish itself. Try using the sentence starts in this entry as word associations— put your pen to paper and complete the sentence starts without putting too much thought into them. You may be surprised at the answers you give. This is one more way to free up your ability to express your feelings.

Letting it out and letting go are parts of a process in which people learn how to cope with and manage difficult feelings so that they can use these as a basis for emotional stability and personal growth.

LETTING IT OUT

1. *The reality of job loss is like . . .* _____

_____

2. *When I learned I'd lost my job, I felt . . .* _____

_____

3. *The first time I told anyone I'd been fired, I felt . . .* _____

_____

4. *I still feel . . .* _____

5. Complete each of the following sentences. *My emotions feel like . . .*

the seasons coming and going because _____

_____

a complicated puzzle because _____

_____

physical pain because _____

_____

a broken vase because _____

_____

a raging river because _____

_____

6. Describe how you are feeling right now.

_____

_____

_____

7. *If this feeling . . .*

had a color it would be _____

had a sound it would be _____

had a texture it would be _____

THINGS TO THINK ABOUT

- What was it like describing feelings? Was it easy or hard?
- Was it difficult or easy to let go of feelings? Were you able to be honest about your feelings?
- Is this sort of emotional letting go useful? Do you need to keep letting go? Will you use this format again to continue writing about your feelings?

Dealing with Reality

One way or another, the reality of losing your job stinks! But, earlier in the chapter it was stated that demoralization, panic, and insecurity are not *necessary* by-products of job loss. How *you* deal with this reality is very much about you, and not the loss itself. In fact, the way you approach recovery will be connected directly with the way you approach life in general. Even though this book and your work in it are prompted by and built upon your job loss, everything in your journal is about *you*. Consequently, how you deal with reality has much to do with how you define that reality.

Friedrich Nietzsche said "that which does not kill me makes me stronger." Is this true for you? Use this final journal entry to think about the impact of this loss on you, what you've learned from your journal entries in this chapter, and how to move on from here.

Demoralization, panic, and insecurity are not necessary by-products of job loss. How you deal with this reality is very much about you, and not the loss itself.

CHECKPOINT: DEALING WITH REALITY

1. *Loss . . .*

__damages my self confidence.

__humiliates me.

__sets me free.

__hurts my pride.

__frightens me.

__helps me value life.

__pushes me in new directions.

__humbles me.

__makes me feel vulnerable.

__frustrates me.

__helps me value family and friends.

__makes me stronger.

other: _____ _____

_____ _____

2. Look at the answers you just checked off or added.

a. Which answer is the most true for you right now?_____

b. Which answer would you like to be the most true? _____

3. How have you dealt with difficult situations in the past?

_____

_____

_____

_____

_____

4. What makes this situation so tough?

_____

_____

_____

_____

_____

5. Name three difficult things to let go of along your journey to self-renewal.

a. _____

b. _____

c. _____

6. What's it like to have to let go of these things?

_____

_____

_____

7. "Will's and won'ts" represent your commitment to stay emotionally and physically healthy. Think about each one before you check off your agreement.

a. __I *will* stay active in my daily life.

b. __I *will* be patient with myself.

c. __I *will* connect with others.

d. __I *will* express my feelings.

e. __I *will* take care of my physical health.

f. __I *will* seek support if I need it.

a. __I *won't* expect people to know how I'm feeling if I don't tell them.

b. __I *won't* try to hide my feelings.

c. __I *won't* try to predict how long it will take to feel better.

d. __I *won't* isolate myself.

e. __I *won't* make any major decisions.

f. __I *won't* try to escape from my feelings.

8. *Right now, I feel . . .* _____

_____

_____

_____

9. *Now I need to . . .* _____

_____

_____

_____

THINGS TO THINK ABOUT

- Does adversity make you grow stronger or weaker? When you're weak do you have people you can turn to for support? When you're strong, do you recognize the needs of others who may need your help?

- Is adversity of this sort new for you, or is this just one more challenge to deal with? What's helped when dealing with difficult situations in the past? If this is a new experience, do you need to get some help?

- Was it difficult to agree with the "will's and won'ts"? Are you really ready to follow their suggestions as you work your way through your recovery and renewal?

4

Destination:

ADJUSTING TO THE SITUATION

"*People don't choose their careers; they are engulfed by them.*"
—JOHN DOS PASSOS

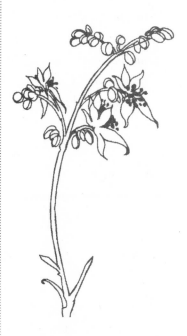

THOMAS

It was bad enough no longer being the vice president in charge of finance. But as a crowning blow, I became the chief cook and bottle washer for the family. My children complained about my cooking, and my wife complained about the way I washed the dishes.

MAUREEN

I went from this dizzying world of appointments and meetings, phone calls, decision making and planning, and more meetings to a strange world where it didn't really matter what I did that day, or even the day after. Even if it was a crazy world I worked in, it was structured and I had a clearly defined place in it. And, although I hate to admit it, having such a critical place in my job made me feel important.

Except I realize now that I didn't have such a critical place at work after all, and I wasn't really important. I was replaced almost at once, and my job just disappeared overnight. Now I'm figuring out how to deal with being out of work, how to feel important even without a job, and how to use my time in a way that's productive and rewarding. It's all very frustrating and worrisome, but I think I'm starting to adjust to all the changes. I'm starting to think that there's more to life than schedules and spreadsheets.

THERE ARE MANY things that will change after being laid off besides your feelings. Job loss changes your financial status, your sense of structure and pace, and the amount of free time you have. If you have a family, job loss changes your relationship with your partner and children. Job loss also changes your perception of yourself and your place in the world.

Adjusting to Change

Adjustment is an immediate issue, something that has to happen first in order to successfully take care of long-term goals later. The actual tasks of adjustment have little to do with resolving major issues, handling all problems, or making major life decisions. Rather, adjustment involves your ability to accommodate this new set of circumstances and regulate your life around your new situation and schedule. Ideally, it means not just accepting and adapting to change and stopping there, but creating a new—even if temporary—lifestyle that is productive and emotionally rewarding.

Adjustment involves your ability to accommodate this new set of circumstances and regulate your life around your new situation and schedule.

This period of adjustment and acclimation to job loss is more than just a stopgap measure. It's an early step along your journey of rebuilding and self-renewal. During this period, your experiences will not only set the stage for your job search, but will help to define what's important, what you want out of your life, and what you want and need from future work. A healthy adjustment is an important step in your journey. For now, the goal is adjustment to your situation—a situation you *cannot* easily change at this time.

The Process of Adjustment

Some people are able to adjust to change easily, while some people struggle to adjust. Adjustment isn't really a thing you do; rather, it's a process that involves several components.

- Adjustment first requires *acknowledging* that change has happened and is quite probably outside of your control. People in denial of the facts or who are unable to acknowledge what's happened or how they're feeling face great difficulty transitioning to this new part of their life.

- *Accommodation* means accepting the change into your life; it doesn't mean welcoming, liking, or agreeing with change. Those who constantly lash out angrily or can't get used to changes in their lives are likely to experience ongoing discomfort and disappointment and aren't likely to find ways to make use of this experience.

- *Adapting* is key to survival. Adapting means making the necessary changes in *yourself* to work with and survive change in your environment—learning to work with change, rather than against it. Those unable to change themselves to fit new circumstances may not prove resilient enough to meet the challenges of the world that has changed around them.

Those unable to change themselves to fit new circumstances may not prove resilient enough to meet the challenges of the world that has changed around them.

Use the next journal entry to think about adjustment and how you're dealing with each of these different elements. Like all of the journal entries in *The Healing Journey Through Job Loss*, this entry asks you to think about your responses as honestly and directly as you can.

ACKNOWLEDGMENT, ACCOMMODATION, AND ADAPTATION

1. Describe five things that are difficult to adjust to.

a. _____

b. _____

c. _____

d. _____

e. _____

2. Acknowledgment

a. What most needs to be acknowledged at this time in your life?

__I feel I have no one to turn to for help.   __I feel that this was my fault.

__I feel that I've let down my family.   __I feel worthless.

__I have to ask for help to deal with this.   __I'm afraid I won't be able to find work.

__I'm anxious about being unemployed.   __I have many negative feelings.

__I feel I didn't do my job well enough.   __I was fired.

__I wasn't important enough.   __I wasn't prepared.

__I'm afraid people will think I'm a loser.   __I'm unemployed.

other: _____   _____

_____   _____

b. *I can best acknowledge my job loss by . . .* _____

_____

_____

_____

2. Accommodation

a. What are the most difficult things to accept?

_____

_____

_____

b. What are the most difficult things to get used to?

_____

_____

c. *It's really difficult to admit that . . .* _____

_____

_____

d. *I can better accommodate this situation by . . .* _____

_____

_____

3. Adaptation

a. What are the most difficult things to adapt to?

__admitting this happened   __all the free time

__being alone more of the time   __feeling disempowered

__feeling useless   __getting used to being home all day

__having less money   __having nothing to do

__having to do things I don't want to do   __having to look for a job

__having to "sell" myself   __new relationships with my family

__not having a job to go to every day   __telling people I don't have a job

other: _____   _____

_____   _____

_____

b. *I most need to adapt to . . .* _____

_____

_____

c. *I most need to adapt by . . .* _____

_____

_____

d. What might help increase you ability to adapt to this situation?

_____

_____

_____

_____

THINGS TO THINK ABOUT

- Can you use this period of unemployment to take on projects, tasks, or interests that you've been trying to time find for? Is there a way to make this period productive in other ways, besides finding a new job?
- In your adjustment to job loss, how important is your family as a source of support and encouragement?
- Do you feel stuck, unable to deal with this new situation? Do you need some help figuring out how to get unstuck?

Personal Style and Adjustment

Adjustment is both something that you do and something that happens to you.

Your ability to adjust well to significant change is important. But it isn't as simple as just making up your mind to adjust and then getting on with it. If life were that straightforward, then a simple pep talk would be enough to convince most people of what to do and how to do it and get them to overcome every obstacle.

Adjustment is both something that you *do* and something that happens *to* you. In the first case, in response to an external situation you make the appropriate changes in your behavior and attitude. In the second, you undergo a psychological change that allows you to operate effectively within the new situation. It's this second aspect of adjustment that's so critical. Without *internal* flexibility, its difficult to make *external* change.

It's true that personal adjustment can be encouraged and fostered through supportive relationships and counseling. Nevertheless, adjustment is a task influenced by the interplay of four underlying personal factors:

- *Psychological processes* are the way you feel and think about and experience the world, both consciously and unconsciously. Your ability to adjust is tied to your ability to understand and, if necessary, change the way you think.

- *Emotional connections* are the relationships you form with people and things and the way these relationship bonds affect you. Adjustment usually means disconnecting from those emotional ties that limit and hold you back and developing emotionally satisfying connections that help you move toward your goals.

- *Flexibility* is your ability to "roll with the punches." Adjustment is built on the ability to recognize and adapt to changes in the environment, and it's reflected in a lifestyle redesigned to accommodate changes.

- *Integrative skills* are your ability to develop and live a life in which you've accommodated and incorporated change, so you are able to exert more control over the way you live your life. Here the key lies in being able to integrate your experiences, using them as the basis for a new perception of reality, or the renewal of your life.

Adjustment is built on the ability to recognize and adapt to changes in the environment, and it's reflected in a lifestyle redesigned to accommodate changes.

At this point in your life, the issues really aren't about *whether* to change or *why* you should have to change. The current task is about *how* to change and what interferes with the ability to adapt to the reality of the change that's swept through your life.

EXPLORING ADJUSTMENT

1. In general, how well have you adjusted to your job loss?

_____

_____

_____

_____

2. What has this change been like for you?

_____

_____

_____

_____

3. What sort of difficulties do you typically have with change and adjustment?

_____

_____

_____

_____

4. What most affects your ability to accept and adjust to this change in your life?

_____

_____

_____

_____

5. *Difficulties to adjustment are mostly . . .*

__personality. I don't like the idea that I have to make any changes at all.

__emotional. The changes are emotionally overwhelming.

__practical. I don't have the financial or other resources required for change.

other: _____

_____

6. *The three things most interfering with my ability to adjust are . . .*

a. _____

b. _____

c. _____

7. Look back at what you've written so far. Is there a pattern or theme to what's most getting in the way of adjusting to this change?

_____

_____

_____

_____

8. *Some things I can do to help me get over these hurdles to adjustment are . . .*

_____

_____

_____

_____

_____

THINGS TO THINK ABOUT

- Were you able to recognize circumstances or personal attributes that are affecting your ability to adjust? Did you learn anything surprising about yourself?
- Were you able to identify any specific ways to more effectively deal with adjustment problems?
- How important is it that you manage to accommodate these changes?

Thinking outside of the Lines

There are different kinds of journal entries throughout this book. All are designed to help you loosen up your thinking and step outside of the normal processes of your daily life. But there are

Journal-writing exercises built on humor, art, contemplation, and relaxation provide other vehicles for seeing things from a new perspective.

many different ways to expand imagination and creativity and thus gain insights into the world around you and yourself. Journal-writing exercises built on humor, art, contemplation, and relaxation provide other vehicles for seeing things from a new perspective.

Creative people think outside of the lines that make up our lives. They manage to step to one side and see the world from a different angle, in a different light, or as an interesting composition of shapes, textures, and contrasts. In this way, we not only learn more about ourselves and our environment, but the world becomes a more interesting place. In this next journal entry you'll create an acrostic poem, which, when rearranged, will give new meaning to your feelings about being fired.

AN ANAGRAM OF FEELINGS

1. Write one sentence about your job loss, your former employer, or your current experience in general, beginning with each of the following letters.

F _____

A _____

D _____

I _____

F _____

L _____

O _____

2. Is there a general theme to your poem, or do the sentiments change with each sentence?

_____

_____

_____

3. What does what you've written say about your feelings?

_____

_____

_____

_____

4. Did you give much thought to each sentence before writing it, or did you just dash off whatever came to mind? Why?

_____

_____

_____

_____

5. Now rearrange your poem, exactly as you've written it, into this order.

L _____

A _____

I _____

D _____

O _____

F _____

F _____

6. Read your poem. Imagine that someone else has written it. What would you say about this poem?

_____

_____

_____

_____

7. What would you infer about the author of the poem?

_____

_____

_____

8. What does the poem tell you about your reaction to being laid off?

_____

_____

_____

_____

9. Do you want to write another acrostic poem?

F _____

I _____

R _____

E _____

D _____

THINGS TO THINK ABOUT

- Did this journal entry seem silly, liberating, odd, important, or difficult? Was it valuable or meaningless? Why?
- Is there anyone you can share this poem with? What might he or she say about it?
- Were you surprised by the way the poem read once you rearranged it? Did you learn anything about yourself from this entry? Do you want to revise this acrostic poem? Will you try to write other acrostic poems?

Recalling the Day

By now you're more aware of how you're feeling, how your job loss has affected you, and how you're responding to being unemployed. One step in addressing and adjusting to difficult, and even traumatic, situations is describing the event. Although you've been doing this throughout this chapter in one way or another, it will be important to have a record of what happened the day you lost your job. The next journal entry tells the story of that day. It may be enough to record the details in this way, or you may later want to write a more complete account of the day you lost your job and the events that led up it.

THAT DAY

1. Tell the story of how you lost you job.

a. *I started this job on . . .* _____

b. *I lost my job on . . .* _____

c. *I lost my job because . . .* _____

_____

_____

2. How did you find out you'd been fired?

_____

_____

3. How did you react to the news?

_____

_____

_____

_____

4. What did you do immediately after finding out you'd lost your job?

_____

_____

_____

_____

5. Describe your reactions and responses during the twenty-four hours immediately following your job loss.

_____

_____

_____

_____

_____

6. Have you ever been fired before? If you have, how did those previous experiences affect the way you felt this time? If you haven't, what was it like to be initiated into the world of fired employees?

_____

_____

_____

_____

_____

7. What would like to say about being fired?

_____

_____

_____

_____

_____

8. What would you like to say to or tell your former employers?

_____

_____

_____

_____

_____

- Is it important to tell the story of your job loss? Are there any family members or friends who need to hear this story?
- Is yours a bitter story, a sad story, or a resigned story? Did the way you told the story capture your feelings about losing your job? Should you rewrite the story so it better expresses your feelings?
- Do you have many unexpressed feelings about being fired? If so, how will you be able to relieve yourself of these feelings?

Reviewing Your Situation

As you finish this chapter, take the time to reflect back on the work you've completed so far. This last entry will allow you the opportunity to think about and summarize your adjustment. If you find yourself stuck—unable to accept what has happened, adjust to this new situation, or figure out how to move on—it will be important to get an outside perspective.

If you find yourself stuck—unable to accept what has happened, adjust to this new situation, or figure out how to move on—it will be important to get an outside perspective.

If you haven't already shared your thoughts and feelings with your family and friends, you're not only missing valuable support, but also an important outside point of view. You also deprive your family of the opportunity to share with you their experience of job loss and adjustment difficulties they may be facing.

Job loss can sometimes lead to depression, anxiety, stress reactions, anger, and other powerful feelings and moods. These often result in difficulty sleeping, decreased appetite, loss of pleasure or interest, diminished energy, problems with concentration and memory, panic attacks, and even thoughts of self-harm or harm to others. If you find your emotions overwhelming, consult with your primary care physician or a mental health professional.

CHECKING IN WITH YOURSELF

1. Think about your job loss and present situation.

a. What most disturbs you about your job loss?

_____

_____

b. What most disturbs you about the way you lost your job?

_____

_____

c. What aspect of job loss has been the most difficult to *adjust* to?

_____

_____

d. What aspect of job loss has been the most difficult to *accept*?

_____

_____

2. Think about your emotions and behavior responses.

a. How well have you been handling your emotions?

_____

_____

b. What most helps when you're feeling upset or emotionally overwrought?

_____

_____

c. What sort of behaviors should you avoid when feeling upset?

_____

_____

3. If you have a family, in what way has job loss most affected family life?

_____

_____

4. If you've already completed Chapter 3 ("Destination: Dealing with Reality"), think back to the "Return on Your Investment" journal entry. If you haven't already completed that entry, go back and do it now. What *gains* have been introduced into your life through your job loss?

_____

_____

_____

5. Consider your overall adjustment to job loss.
a. Are you making a healthy adjustment?

_____

_____

_____

b. What most stands in the way of a healthy adjustment?

_____

_____

_____

c. What might help ease or improve your adjustment?

_____

_____

_____

THINGS TO THINK ABOUT

- Are you sharing your experience with family and friends? Are you allowing them to help and support you? Do you feel this is your burden alone to bear?
- Are you having a particularly difficult time with adjustment? Do you need some help getting through this or figuring out what to do next? Who can you turn to for emotional, professional, or practical support?
- Are you able to recognize the benefits of a period of unemployment and use these to strengthen you as you recover and rebuild?

5

Destination:

SELF-ESTEEM

MIKE

After I lost my job, my self-esteem plunged through the floor—but not right away. At first I was just embarrassed, and that was hard enough to deal with. Finding the words to tell my wife I'd been asked to resign was really hard, and then I had to tell my kids. Explaining it to them was hard because of their age, and they asked me if that meant the people at work didn't like me. Of course, I told them that it was really okay and everyone still liked me, but their questions really hit a nerve because that's exactly what it felt like. Telling my friends was the next ordeal, and then the neighbors, until it felt like the whole world knew. My ears felt red all the time.

But I got through all that, as tough as it was. The real blow to my self-image came later with the rejection letters and failed interviews, as weeks turned into months. I learned firsthand what it means when they say "Don't call us, we'll call you." Maybe I just got numb to it, or maybe it was having my family and friends believe in me, but I recovered my self-esteem. It's different now, though. In some ways my self-image is even stronger that when I started out,

but I'm also a lot more humble now. I've sure learned a lot from this, especially about myself.

Our sense of personal identity and self-worth —the way we see ourselves—provides the foundation upon which we make decisions, solve problems, take actions, and interact with other people.

THE JOURNAL ENTRIES in this chapter address one of the pivotal issues in job loss—the effects of work, job loss, and unemployment on self-image, self-esteem, and personal identity.

There are many important issues in people's lives once they've been laid off. Practical concerns, financial realities, restructured personal relationships, problem solving, and planning for the future. In many ways the issues of self-esteem underlie almost everything else. Our sense of personal identity and self-worth—the way we see ourselves—provides the foundation upon which we make decisions, solve problems, take actions, and interact with other people.

The work in this chapter is not intended to end when you complete the chapter. Like all the journal entries in this book, the idea is to provide you with tools and journal formats to use repeatedly to examine your feelings, understand yourself, and plan and live your life. Work through this chapter, but use what you learn as the foundation for a continued exploration of self-esteem. The Chinese philosopher Lao-tzu taught that "going on means going far. Going far means returning." Similarly, the poet T. S. Eliot tells us: "We shall not cease from exploration and the end of all our exploring will be to arrive where we started and know the place for the first time."

The Symbolic Meaning of Work

Work doesn't hold personal significance for everyone. For many people, work is no more than a means to an end, and in some cases quite unimportant. Not everyone works, and not everyone chooses to work. Similarly, for some people, job loss is an inconvenience that may or may not lead to financial difficulties but is not a cause for emotional distress. Although prolonged unemployment may ultimately lead to emotional stress because of financial worries, it may not have *any* debilitating effects on self-image, personal direction, or sense of identity. Regardless, the issues of work, job loss, and unemployment are, or have become, central for *you*. And despite the fact that not everyone is seriously affected by job loss, your feelings, doubts, and worries are nevertheless not unusual.

Furthermore, despite *personal* attitudes, *social* attitudes are clear. Under normal circumstances, people are *expected* to be working. People who are unemployed and perceived as not interested in working are often judged as lazy, shiftless, unworthy, or as dependents living off welfare. Social expectations can become one more potential drain on emotional energy and self-image. If you can't find a job, you may fear that your family, friends, or community will begin to see *you* as one of the good-for-nothing unemployed.

In this next journal entry, think about your *general* expectations of and experiences with "work." That is, don't focus on your lost job in particular, but consider the *idea* of work and your work experiences in general. This entry will help you begin thinking about the connection between work and self-esteem.

"We shall not cease from exploration and the end of all our exploring will be to arrive where we started and know the place for the first time."
—T. S. ELIOT

THE MEANING OF WORK

1. What does *work* mean to you? Check all that apply, and add other thoughts.

__a creative outlet

__a dreadful task to be tolerated

__a way to feel good about myself

__a necessary evil

__a way to contribute to society

__a critical function of society

__a means to keep people occupied

__a means of self-expression

__a satisfying way to use my time

__a way to earn money

___a means for some people to exploit others

___a way to get together with other people

___a way to give meaning to my life

___a way to help others

___a way to produce something that others want

___a way to structure my life

other: _____   _____

_____   _____

_____   _____

2. How much does work . . .

a. define the way you *feel* about yourself *(self-esteem)*?

_____

_____

b. influence the way you *see* yourself *(self-image)*?

_____

_____

c. shape your sense of your place in society *(personal identity)*?

_____

_____

3. *Work to me is* . . . _____

_____

_____

_____

4. What has job loss meant?

___loss of dignity   ___loss of faith   ___loss of family   ___loss of identity

___loss of income   ___loss of meaning   ___loss of prestige ___loss of structure

other: _____   _____

_____   _____

5. *Job loss has meant . . .* _____

_____

_____

_____

6. What sort of impact is unemployment having on your life?

___affects my relationships   ___depresses me

___emotionally draining   ___financial

___makes me feel employers don't care   ___makes me question my career choices

___makes me anxious about my future   ___makes me doubt myself

other: _____   _____

_____   _____

7. What are the three most important consequences of your unemployment?

a. _____ because _____

b. _____ because _____

c. _____ because _____

8. *Unemployment has meant . . .* _____

_____

_____

_____

_____

THINGS TO THINK ABOUT

- Is this just a case of being out of work where things will return to "normal" once you return to work? What changes in *you* are unlikely to return to normal even once you begin a new job?
- Has this experience affected the way you see yourself? Has it affected the way you think about work?

- Can you derive meaning out of life outside of work? Have you invested *too* much of yourself into work? Has work influenced *too* much in your life?
- Is this experience having an impact on the way you see your family or they see you? What sort of impact?

Self-Concept

Self-esteem equals self-worth, or how you feel *about yourself. People with high self-esteem have personal regard. High self-esteem helps people tolerate difficult times and face lack of success without emotionally crumbling.*

People most often refer to their self-esteem or self-image when describing how they feel about or see themselves. In the previous journal entry you addressed the impact of work on three *different* aspects of your self-concept: self-esteem, self-image, and personal identity. Together, these three components of the personality form self-concept, or *selfhood*. When people use the expressions *self-esteem* or *self-image*, they're usually referring to a more complex interrelationship between three different aspects of self-concept.

- *Self-esteem equals self-worth, or how you* feel *about yourself.* People with high self-esteem have personal regard. That is, they feel pretty good about themselves. High self-esteem helps people tolerate difficult times and face lack of success without emotionally crumbling. People with low self-esteem tend to feel badly about themselves. In many cases, they might say they don't like themselves.

- *Self-image is a reflection of how you* see *yourself.* People with positive self-image think of themselves as reasonably effective and capable, as someone others would want to know. On the other hand, people with a negative self-image see themselves as incapable and perhaps undesirable.

- *Personal identity captures* who *you are or the way you view your role in the world and your relationships with others.* Your sense of identity is built upon the things you do, your impact on the world, and your perception of your value to others.

People with poorly defined identities often are confused about what's important to them, their personal relationships, and the value to others of the things they do.

Problems with Self-Concept

Although success and satisfaction in a career can significantly contribute to a *healthy* self-concept, the opposite is only partially true. Job loss can (and often does) challenge self-esteem, attack self-image, and erode personal confidence. But job loss alone isn't likely to result in the complete collapse of a healthy self-concept. Indeed, it may not challenge self-esteem at all. You may have a strong and well-developed enough sense of self to withstand this emotional challenge, no matter how exacting. In fact, significant problems in self-concept often predate job loss, although the loss will certainly aggravate the problem.

Regardless of origin, low self-esteem, negative self-image, or confused personal identity can be serious problems. A negative or uncertain sense of self often equals a sense of incompetence, inadequacy, or helplessness. This can easily result in emotional problems and an impaired ability to function effectively. If you're experiencing significant emotional difficulties or feel that your self-concept is being crushed, consult with your primary care physician or a mental health practitioner. You may find that counseling or therapy can contribute to the development of a healthier self-concept.

The next journal entry is entirely focused on the way you see yourself. If you find some of your answers difficult to deal with, it may simply signal the beginning of a new openness with yourself. Because self-esteem, self-image, and personal identity change over time, this may be an entry that you'll want to return to periodically and check in with yourself. Be sure to photocopy the blank entry before you use it for the first time.

A negative or uncertain sense of self often equals a sense of incompetence, inadequacy, or helplessness.

WHEN I THINK OF MYSELF . . .

1. Self-Esteem

a. Circle the number that most approximates your sense of self regard, where 1 equals feeling pretty lousy about yourself and 5 equals feeling pretty great.

Low Self-Esteem			High Self-Esteem	
I really feel bad about myself.			*I really feel good about myself.*	
1	2	3	4	5

b. Explain your rating. How do you *feel* about yourself, and why?

_____

_____

_____

_____

2. Self-Image

a. How positive is your self-image? Again, circle the number that comes closest to describing how you see yourself, where 1 equals a negative self-image and 5 represents a positive self-image.

Negative Self-Image			Positive Self-Image	
I see myself as really ineffective.			*I see myself as really effective.*	
1	2	3	4	5

b. Explain your answer. How do you *see* yourself, and why?

_____

_____

_____

_____

3. Personal Identity

How clear is your sense of personal identity? Again, 1 equals an uncertain or shaky sense of identity and unclear role and 5 equals clarity of your role and sharpness of identity.

Confused and Uncertain Identity   Clear and Certain Identity

I'm confused or uncertain about my role.   *I'm clear and certain about my role.*

1   2   3   4   5

b. Explain your answer. In what ways do you experience confusion or clarity about who you are as a person, both in terms of identity and role?

_____

_____

_____

_____

_____

4. How much does work . . .

a. affect the way you feel about yourself (*self-esteem*)?_____

_____

_____

b. influence the way you see yourself (*self-image*)?_____

_____

_____

c. define your place in society (*personal identity*)?_____

_____

_____

_____

5. What *is* your overall self-concept? How do you generally see yourself?

_____

_____

_____

_____

6. How much has job loss affected your overall self-concept?

_____

_____

_____

_____

7. What's changed the most in your self-concept since job loss? Why?

_____

_____

_____

_____

8. What's been the most difficult part of maintaining a healthy self-concept since losing your job and why?

_____

_____

_____

_____

9. How are you feeling as you complete this entry?

_____

_____

_____

_____

- Whatever your sense of self—positive or negative, strong or weak—how do others see you? Do you think they agree with your self-evaluation? Do you know? How can you find out? Do you *want* to find out?
- How do you judge yourself—strong or weak, effective or ineffective? Do you understand why you evaluate yourself this way? What sort of things diminish your self-image, and what sort of things strengthen it?
- How important is self-concept in building your life and moving forward? Can you succeed without a positive opinion of yourself? If not, how can you begin to build positive self-image?

Building Self-Esteem

Your ability to deal with this crisis in your life will, to some degree, be built upon your sense of self-esteem, self-image, and personal identity. These three aspects of selfhood tend to blur together and mirror and influence one another. Therefore, building strength in any one area will result in an increase in every aspect of self-concept. Experiencing a sense of personal success increases self-esteem. You will like yourself, you will feel worthy, and you will feel empowered. These things lead to improved self-image, in which you feel effective and capable of success. In turn, this sort of inner confidence provides the basis for self-assured decision making and increases your sense of personal identity and ability to interact effectively with the world.

Your ability to deal with this crisis in your life will, to some degree, be built upon your sense of self-esteem, self-image, and personal identity.

Not everyone, however, holds themselves in high regard in the first place. It's important to do things that support and build self-esteem in order to get through a time in your life where your sense of self is under attack. Unfortunately, like so many things that have to do with emotions, you can't simply pep-talk yourself into positive self-esteem. It's a condition you develop over time.

Recognizing Success and Accomplishment

One way to build self-esteem is to experience success. In order to experience success, you first have to recognize it when it happens to you. People who recognize personal success are able to use it as a platform upon which to develop other successes. These, in turn, lead to a sense of personal accomplishment, self-satisfaction, and empowerment, and thus self-esteem is born or sustained.

People define for themselves the meaning of success and failure.

Success is also like money in the bank: it builds interest. If you've experienced success, you can afford failure and can tolerate it. Failure isn't something that totally wipes you out, because you have a success "nest egg" to keep you going. People who only experience failure find failure more difficult to bear. They may not even recognize personal success when it's staring them in the face. Of course, it's not necessarily true that "successful" people can tolerate failure. Just as success is a state of mind, so too is failure. People define for themselves the meaning of success and failure.

You can think of the opposite of success as failure. In a black-and-white world that might be true, but we don't live in a such a world, if it exists anywhere. In the real world, not succeeding isn't necessarily the same as failing (unless you define it that way or allow others to define it that way for you). Often the opposite of success isn't failure but is more simply a lack of success. Ever practical and realistic, Winston Churchill once noted that "success is maintaining enthusiasm between failures." In the real world, success, lack of success, and failure are not clear-cut concepts. In fact, there are often many levels of success and many ways to define it.

In this context, although losing your job can't be considered success, it doesn't equal failure. This is a way to put your experiences

—positive and negative—into a context that allows personal growth, not personal defeat. Think about successes, failures, and lack of success in your life and the meaning of each. Are there other ways to define success and accomplishment? Now consider this simple equation:

$$\text{Self-Esteem} = \frac{\text{Accomplishment}}{\text{Expectations}}$$

This formula suggests that self-esteem is the product of accomplishment divided by expectations. In this case, one way to increase self-esteem is to increase accomplishments or successes. Another is to reduce expectations. How does this idea have bearing in your life at a time when self-esteem is so critical?

ACCOMPLISHMENTS OVER EXPECTATIONS

1. What sort of expectations do you have for yourself?

_____

_____

_____

2. Can you reduce expectations without feeling that you're somehow lowering your standards?

_____

_____

_____

3. Would reducing expectations also reduce pressure on you? Why or why not?

_____

_____

_____

4. What sort of expectations do others have of you?

_____

_____

_____

5. Describe five ways in which you could reasonably reduce expectations placed on you by yourself or others:

a. _____

b. _____

c. _____

d. _____

e. _____

6. Are there different types of accomplishments besides getting a new job? Use this "tickler" list to stretch your mind into considering other types of success. Check off any that you see as accomplishments or things you'd like to accomplish; then add ten more items of your own. Be as specific as possible.

__being a good parent	__building a new career	__developing a hobby
__getting fit	__exploring nature	__growing a garden
__having a good marriage	__learning a new skill	__learning to play guitar
__learning to relax	__pressing flowers	__reading a book
__running a support group	__spending time with family	__spending time with friends
__taking up art	__volunteer work	__writing a book

other: _____   _____

_____   _____

_____   _____

_____   _____

_____   _____

7. How can you increase your accomplishments without returning to work?

_____

_____

_____

Self-Esteem and Relationships

Self-esteem is built on more than just concrete goals and your ability to achieve them. It's also built on abstract experiences such as your beliefs about what you can and cannot do, your values, and whether you live up to them. Social relationships also directly feed into self-esteem.

Most people care about and are influenced by the way they're seen by others. And the more important those other people are, the more we care about how we're seen by them. The people in your life aren't just passive objects—they respond to you and what you do. Their reactions help shape your self-image and affect self-esteem. Positive, healthy, and emotionally satisfying relationships boost self-esteem. They provide indirect evidence of your value. Strained, emotionally difficult, and distant relationships with people tend to feed into a negative cycle that limits and drains self-confidence and lowers self-esteem.

Self-esteem is built on more than just concrete goals and your ability to achieve them.

The way that you *think* people see you is also bound to have an effect on you. You may worry that some people will see you as incapable of holding down a job or incompetent or that others will dismiss you as unimportant. You may fear that job loss will reveal your weaknesses to others or make you feel vulnerable and at a disadvantage. The sense of vulnerability and embarrassment only deepens with prolonged unemployment. Similarly, if you've lost more than one job, your feelings of failure and your concerns about public perception may run even stronger.

Use this next entry to think about your relationships with others and how these hinder, help, or generally affect your self-esteem. This entry asks you to discuss with family or friends how they see you. When you reach that point, pause your entry and don't return to it until you're able to complete that particular question.

THE WORLD

1. How do you *want* to be seen, or judged, by others?

_____

_____

_____

_____

2. What are your worst fears about what others might think of you now?

_____

_____

_____

_____

3. What has been the most difficult thing to tell others about how you're feeling or what you're going through?

_____

_____

_____

4. Has it been embarrassing to tell people about your job loss or discuss it with them? If it has, complete the next four sentence starts.

a. *I feel embarrassed because* . . . _____

_____

b. *I feel embarrassed because* . . . _____

_____

c. *I feel embarrassed because* . . . _____

_____

d. *I feel embarrassed because* . . . _____

_____

5. In what ways can the most significant people in your life help you maintain and boost your self-esteem and self-confidence?

_____

_____

_____

_____

_____

6. What do these significant people see as your strengths? Ask five people for a frank evaluation of your most important qualities. For each person, identify one of the important traits they identified in you.

Significant Person	An Important Quality in You
_____	_____
_____	_____
_____	_____
_____	_____
_____	_____

7. How are you affected by the way you're seen by others?

_____

_____

_____

_____

_____

8. How can you draw strength and support from other people?

_____

_____

_____

_____

THINGS TO THINK ABOUT

- If married, do you include your spouse among the most important people in your life? If you have children, do you include them? Have you allowed them to help and support you? If not, how come?
- Were there people that it was especially difficult to tell? Why? Are there people you really wish didn't have to know about this? If so, why?

Self-Affirmation

Behaviors and attitudes that result in success lead to the development of other behaviors and attitudes that are positive.

Nothing builds success like success. Personal achievements lay the groundwork for further accomplishment. Behaviors and attitudes that result in success lead to the development of other behaviors and attitudes that are positive. The reverse is true also. Behaviors and attitudes that are ineffective are often self-defeating or self-destructive. They not only fail to meet goals but often aggravate the situation and create new problems. Disappointment, frustration, and a sense of failure frequently become breeding grounds for still more problem behaviors and attitudes.

It's easy, then, to imagine either a self-*defeating* or self-*affirming* cycle. Low self-esteem, negative self-image, and a confused identity are only to create a chain in which negative experiences in any one area promote negative experiences in the others. In the self-affirming cycle, positive experiences empower and contribute to an overall healthy sense of self.

These cycles are driven in part by the things you do and the relationships you hold. But the glue that holds things together is *perception,* or the way you see things. People who distort their experiences so that everything is seen as a loss, a slap in the face, or a confirmation of a lousy world will have a difficult time finding goodness in anything, including themselves. On the other hand, a willingness to see the positive, even under difficult circumstances, provides the fuel for *self-affirmation,* or the ability to feel good about yourself. Self-affirming thoughts can contribute to an improved sense of self and your capacity to survive difficult times and grow stronger as a result.

For every disappointment and failure in your life, there's almost certainly a satisfying and successful experience waiting to be counted. An *affirmation* is an assertion of a truth, a belief, or an ideal—a way to put out an idea and commit yourself to it. In this case, the affirmation reflects your commitment to *yourself* and your health, goodness, strength, and ability to get through a difficult time in your life.

> "Remember, no one can make you feel inferior without your consent."
> —ELEANOR ROOSEVELT

I AM . . .

1. Name four things of which you're proud. These can include goals you've achieved, special skills, personal relationships, adversity you've overcome, decisions you've made, or a particular role you play in life.

a. _____

b. _____

c. _____

d. _____

2. Now describe four personal qualities about which you feel good. These can include your generosity, the way you look, your sense of humor, being a good spouse or parent, your compassion for issues or empathy for others, your ability to make new friends, or your attitudes and beliefs.

a. _____

b. _____

c. _____

d. _____

3. Complete these sentences.

a. *I know I can deal with difficult times because I . . .*

_____

_____

b. *Although my job loss has thrown me, I . . .*

_____

_____

c. *Above all, I value myself because . . .*

_____

_____

d. *One thought that helps me through difficult times is . . .*

_____

_____

THINGS TO THINK ABOUT

- Was this is a difficult entry for you? Were you able to describe accomplishments or personal qualities of which you're proud? If not, why not? Do you need help figuring out how to feel better about yourself?

- Do self-reinforcing thoughts help you gather internal strength or feel better about yourself during a difficult time?

6

Destination:

SUPPORT

PAUL

I was never out of work in my life until I lost my job at the hospital. I knew right away that I was in trouble. We had big debts that we could cover only as long as I was working at that salary level, and it was pretty clear to me that I'd be lucky to find another job in my field at my old salary. But I felt like I couldn't tell anyone. I couldn't tell my wife because I didn't want to scare her. And because I ran the household, she had no idea how much we owed, and I didn't want her to think I'd botched things up. I couldn't tell my friends because I didn't want them feeling sorry for me, and I didn't want them to know how little we had in the bank.

I felt really trapped and I really needed help. But to be honest, just going down to the unemployment office every week made me feel like I was getting a handout. I wanted to call up everyone I knew and ask for help, but I couldn't do it. It made me feel like I was crawling, and I felt like I needed to keep my head high. And the longer I held on to my pride, the harder it got to ask for help.

I was lucky, because I found a job before I hit rock bottom. Only after that was I able to really tell my wife how worried I'd been and

how scared and lonely I'd felt. To tell you the truth, I felt stupid that I hadn't told her. First of all, it was such a relief to tell someone and unload. Second, she had a right to know. And third, it would have been a lot less lonely to have had someone to talk to along the way. I think I made life a good deal harder for myself by going it alone.

Support comes in many forms, and different kinds of support are needed at different times.

SUPPORT IS A key factor in how well people deal with significant loss or trauma. In fact, it almost goes without saying that people affected by significant events in their lives need emotional support if they're to cope with and move through, and eventually beyond, the trauma.

The loss of a job is sometimes no more than just a bump along the road. Increasingly though, in our marketplace-driven society, we're seeing more and more job losses, bigger bumps along roads that are increasingly rougher for some people, and massive changes in both the job market and the work environment itself. For many, job loss becomes a difficult and even desperate time. Like so many things in our complex and changing society, support is a critical element in recovery and self-renewal. And, as with other circumstances in which support is critical, research supports the idea that people who have support systems following job loss experience less depression and less physical illness than those without such support.

Support comes in many forms, and different kinds of support are needed at different times. The primary focus of this chapter is to help you decide what kind of support is needed and when, and how and from whom you can get it.

Support Networks

Nowadays, when people speak of networking they're referring to the process of reaching out across a network for the specific purpose of getting a job. These sorts of career networks are forms of support, of course, but that's not their primary purpose. But a *support* network or system is made up of people and resources whose *primary* purpose is to provide support. A broad and comprehensive support network will be capable of meeting a variety of needs.

Within any system there are two distinct sources of support. One is typically made up of families, friends, and others in your general community—such as neighbors, acquaintances, and former coworkers. This is a *natural* support system that grows out of your everyday relationships and interactions, composed of people in your life. Once people in this system are aware of your situation, they'll usually want to help in some way.

You also have a secondary support system available, which provides a different kind of help. This is a system of help that's available upon demand, sometimes at no cost and sometimes on a fee-for-service basis. This system usually involves people and organizations that aren't naturally aware of your needs, but have to be alerted to your needs and recruited to help. This *drafted* support system includes vocational training centers and employment agencies, financial institutions, job counselors and mental health providers, accountant, attorneys, labor unions, and religious organizations.

In the natural support system, help can mean many things but is always personal. You're more likely to receive emotional support and help with the practical issues of daily life from your family and friends than you are to find a new job or deal with serious emotional or mental health issues. Conversely, your drafted support system can provide job opportunities, retraining, emotional and spiritual guidance, loans, financial guidance, and legal assistance, but you are unlikely to receive the sort of emotional warmth, concern, and understanding available from family and friends.

There are always exceptions: people find jobs through their natural support system, and it's not unusual to build a strongly supportive relationship with drafted helpers such as clergy and

Within any system there are two distinct sources of support: a natural support system and a drafted support system.

mental health counselors. As a general rule, though, natural and drafted support systems provide different kinds of help. In the drafted system, help is usually of a professional nature and is more likely to be addressed toward the resolution of a particular problem. Natural support is personal, continuous, and doesn't disappear once the situation is resolved.

The Faces of Support

Support is a broad word with many meanings. Basically, though, when thinking about job loss in particular, support can be broken into three primary types: emotional, practical, and professional.

Emotional support often refers to those intangible things that have do with human interactions and relationships. This sort of support includes someone to talk to and acts of kindness and generosity that let you know that you're personally valued and aren't just a number or a statistic. Emotional support is usually a function of your natural support system.

Practical support is usually based on concrete needs. It includes things like financial assistance, help in managing your daily life (like child care, if you're a single parent), and job leads. Practical help can come from your natural or drafted support network.

Professional support is typically focused on tasks directly associated with getting a job or dealing with issues directly related to your situation. This sort of support includes professional employment searches, resume preparation, vocational training, and job counseling. It might also include legal representation, financial planning, and mental health counseling. You're likely to get this kind of help only from your system of drafted support.

Whether emotional, practical, or professional, support provides a safety net and a lifeline to help you get back up. It provides the emotional security of knowing you have people on your side and in your corner.

Emotional support is usually a function of your natural support system.

In the next journal entry, think about your support system. Who's in it? Is it lopsided, providing only one kind of support when you're likely to need more than one type?

ASSESSING SUPPORT

1. Who's available to you for support?

_____

_____

_____

_____

2. What kind of support are you getting?

_____

_____

_____

_____

3. Is it the right kind of support? Why or why not?

_____

_____

_____

_____

4. Do people know you need support?

_____

_____

5. Do people know what *kind* of support you need?

_____

_____

6. What kind of support do you most need now?

___emotional   ___practical   ___professional   ___financial

other: _____

7. Name four people or sources of support in each area. It's okay if the same names appear under each different category.

	Emotional	Practical	Professional	Financial
a.	_____	_____	_____	_____
b.	_____	_____	_____	_____
c.	_____	_____	_____	_____
d.	_____	_____	_____	_____

8. Were you able to name five sources for support in each area? Is your support system broad enough to meet your needs in each of these areas?

_____

_____

9. How can you expand your current support system to get more of the support you most need or get unfilled needs met?

_____

_____

_____

_____

THINGS TO THINK ABOUT

- Are you getting the kind of support you need in each area? Do you *need* support in each area?
- What *type* of support has been the most important? Are getting enough support of this type? If not, why not?
- What's the greatest obstacle to getting the kind(s) of support you most need? What can you do to overcome this obstacle?

Getting Support

Support isn't a static thing, and neither is your need for support. At any given time you probably need more than one kind of support, and your needs will vary from day to day and will change over time. For this reason, sometimes support doesn't help. It's well intentioned and it's valuable, but it's the wrong kind of support at the wrong time. The key to getting the *right* kind of support at the *right* time is knowing what kind of support you need and when you need it. You also have to know who to get it from and how. There are several critical factors at play.

The key to getting the right kind of support at the right time is knowing what kind of support you need and when you need it.

- Do people *realize* you need help? The fact is that people don't always ask for support, instead expecting people to *know* that they need help. This is a surefire way to feel disappointed, let down, and disregarded. It's important to realize that people aren't mind readers and don't always know you need support.

- People in your system may not realize *how* much help you need, or the *type* of help most needed. People are often judged by the way they present themselves to others. If you present yourself as resilient and able to handle any crisis, people aren't likely to know that you need more help than you're letting on. People may take you seriously and assume you're okay when you're not okay. Alternatively, people may offer *lots* of support, but it may not be the kind you need at that time. Being honest with people and asking for the kind of support you most need are the best ways to get the support you need.

- Can you can get the type of help you *most* need from your current support system? Bearing in mind that you'll need more than one type of help, you have to assess whether your support system is adequate. No matter how concerned

Being honest with people and asking for the kind of support you most need are the best ways to get the support you need.

or well meaning your current systems are, you'll likely need a support network that can provide the right kind of help at the right time. In fact, it's quite common for people to look for the *right* things in the *wrong* places. This means expecting one type of support from someone who's unable to provide that type of help. This is a setup for failure, disappointment, and perhaps bitterness and frustration.

◆ Will you accept help if it's offered? For many people this is quite difficult. Accepting help is often attached to pride and humility. This is a tough one, and journaling offers a wonderful opportunity to explore these very issues.

The next entry is broad in that it will help you think about asking for and getting support in general. But it's also specific in that it focuses on only a single problem area in which you need some form of help right now. Photocopy the blank format before you use it, and use the entry repeatedly to think about your needs and responses to getting support in every area identified in the first three questions.

SEEING OBSTACLES

1. Name your three greatest practical needs.

a. _____

b. _____

c. _____

2. Name your three greatest emotional needs.

a. _____

b. _____

c. _____

3. Name your three greatest professional needs.

a. _____

b. _____

c. _____

4. Pick one of the needs you named in Questions 1, 2, and 3, and work only on this need for the remainder of this entry. You can repeat the entry later for each of the other needs you've identified. Which need have you chosen for this entry?

_____

5. Name three things that get in the way of being able to ask for help with this need.

a. _____

b. _____

c. _____

6. What is it about *you* that most gets in the way of being more open and honest?

_____

_____

_____

7. How can you overcome obstacles to telling people you need help?

_____

_____

_____

8. List your five greatest fears about *asking* for support.

a. _____

b. _____

c. _____

d. _____

e. _____

9. What's the most difficult part of *accepting* support?

_____

_____

_____

Supportive Relationships

Support not only helps, it also provides some of the fabric out of which self-esteem, self-image, and personal identity are cut. In supportive relationships, support as a means to an end (getting a job) overlaps with support as a way to strengthen yourself (building self-concept). It's important, then, to take time to think about, focus on, and nourish important relationships in your life.

Your natural support system has two tiers: an "outer" circle of neighbors, acquaintances, and colleagues, and an "inner" circle occupied by your closest family and friends.

Your natural support system has two tiers: an "outer" circle of neighbors, acquaintances, and colleagues, and an "inner" circle occupied by your closest family and friends. Nevertheless, some people feel unable to turn to their family or friends for help or don't make clear just how much help may be needed. Relatives and friends are a source of emotional and practical support, and a personal crisis for you offers a chance for your friends to rise to the occasion and prove the old adage, "A friend in need is a friend indeed."

At the same time, family relationships and friendships are quite different in many respects. Although your friends hold a special place in your life and support system, these relationship are different than familial relationships. Friendships are built on mutuality and independence, rather than the *inter*dependence assumed in family relationships. As people age and grow away from the family in which they were raised, family relationships become less intertwined and more independent, often resembling friendships.

As people marry, they're introduced into their "new" family, typically composed of spouses and children. If you're married or have children, support within your family is critical, both in terms of getting and giving support. In many respects, support within a family is a cyclical affair. The most successful families are those in which family members nurture and care for and about one another.

If you have a family, one of your most important tasks is to take care of them financially and emotionally. Is this a one-way street for you, or do you allow them to take care of you as well? Do you include your spouse and other family members in decisions about your life together? Do you ask them how they feel and what they need, without allowing them the opportunity to learn about your feelings and needs?

The next entry will help you think about if and how you get support from your immediate family. You can use the entry to describe relationships within your family of origin if you're unmarried and can easily modify the entry to include any family members who are important in your life. The entry will help you focus on supportive relationships within the family group that you consider to be the most important in your life.

The most successful families are those in which family members nurture and care for and about one another.

FAMILY SUPPORTS

1. Is your immediate family an important source of emotional support? Why or why not?

_____

_____

_____

_____

_____

2. How do you allow your family members to help you through this difficult time?

_____

_____

_____

_____

3. For each member of your immediate family, briefly describe what kind of emotional support you get.

a. *From* _____, *I get* _____

_____

b. *From* _____, *I get* _____

_____

c. *From* _____, *I get* _____

_____

d. *From* _____, *I get* _____

_____

e. *From* _____, *I get* _____

_____

f. *From* _____, *I get* _____

_____

4. Do you owe it to your family to share with them what you're going through at this time and seek their support and involvement? Why or why not?

_____

_____

_____

_____

_____

5. What should you share? What shouldn't you share?

_____

_____

_____

_____

6. What stops you from sharing more with your family?

_____

_____

_____

_____

7. What should you share with your family that you haven't already shared?

_____

_____

_____

_____

_____

- Do you consider what you're going through as a personal problem or a family problem?
- Is it possible that not sharing with your family will cut you off from an important source of support?
- Is it possible that sharing with and getting support from your family can help pull your family closer?

Building a Network of Support

The idea behind a network is that there are *connections* between the different strands in your support system that come together to form a web. Think of a spider's web: It is the *interconnection* that makes the web so tough, durable, and effective, even though each strand may be fragile and inadequate alone.

Perhaps you already have a support network in place, but it's your job to connect your various resources. As you complete the work in this chapter, you enter, or have already entered, the second stage of your journey. Recovering from job loss turns into rebuilding, with the tasks of creating a more stable base for your everyday life. Use this final entry to review your support system and the work that lies ahead in developing your support network so it can best assist you as you rebuild and move on to self-renewal.

CONNECTING THE DOTS

1. Are you satisfied with the amount and type of support you're getting?

_____

_____

_____

_____

_____

2. What are the greatest limitations on the support currently available to you?

_____

_____

_____

_____

_____

3. What areas of your support network most need to be developed?

_____

_____

_____

_____

_____

4. Are you actively building a support network, or are you waiting for one to happen? What steps have you taken?

_____

_____

_____

_____

_____

_____

5. Do you recognize support when it's offered? What are the signs?

_____

_____

_____

_____

_____

_____

6. Do you accept support when it's offered? How do you react?

_____

_____

_____

_____

7. If you have a family:

a. What kind of support does your spouse need from you?

_____

_____

_____

_____

b. What kind of support do your children need from you?

_____

_____

_____

_____

THINGS TO THINK ABOUT

- Is there a difference between support and help? What have you learned about your needs for either?
- Is support a two-way street? Can you *get* support by giving support to others?

7

Destination:
COPING WITH FEELINGS

"There can be no
knowledge without
emotion."
—ARNOLD BENNETT

MARTHA

*I was laid off without notice one afternoon, and I don't think I
ever felt so humiliated in my life. I was actually escorted out of the
building, and I wasn't even allowed to say good-bye to anyone. The
contents of my office were delivered to my home the next day, right
on time and just as my former bosses said they would be. Everything
was so neat for them, and so screwed up for me.*

*It didn't end there. My feelings, I mean—if it wasn't one emo-
tion, it was another. They just kept coming on, one rolling into the
next. The embarrassment of being fired, anger and resentment about
how I'd been treated, worry and anxiety about loss of income, and
fears of not finding another well-paying job. And all those feelings
were spilling over into the rest of my life. I was snapping at the
kids, finding fault with everything my husband did, and losing interest in almost everything. I was smoking heavily, eating less, and
drinking more than usual. Feeling miserable got in the way of
finding another job as well, and I was only halfheartedly looking.
And when I got interviews, I was tired and uninspiring.*

I finally caught on that my feelings had taken on a life all of their own. I can't exactly say that I snapped out of it, because I worked hard to regain control over my feelings. Realizing I was going downhill fast was the first step in getting my life, and my feelings, back together.

EMOTIONS ARE ESSENTIAL ingredients of humanity—we would not be human without them. They're complex and underlie everything we do, forming the foundation for our thoughts. No doubt at this time in your life, your feelings are difficult to deal with. Your emotional picture may be marked by feelings we normally think of as negative—perhaps anger, hostility, bitterness, depression, sadness, and anxiety. Feelings can be overwhelming, and sometimes people want to be rid of their emotions, *especially* when they're unpleasant feelings.

"Individuality is founded in feeling."
—WILLIAM JAMES

Emotions can sometimes lead directly to action. For instance, people often yell without first thinking or cry when they're sad. But, usually *feelings* are followed by *thoughts,* which in turn lead to *behaviors.* Indeed, emotions lay the groundwork for thought, self-knowledge, and personal growth. They provide a beacon that tells us about our reactions to the world and our inner state, if we listen. Feelings, both good and bad, are really important. The work of recovery and rebuilding is never about getting rid of or squashing feelings, but learning how to accept and deal with them. It's what we *do* with them that counts. "Individuality," in the words of William James, "is founded in feeling."

Emotions, Action, and Thought

Outside of your personal experience, an emotion has no independent power to act on the world outside of you. Until an emotion is transformed into an *action,* it's actual impact is neither good nor bad. It's the *behaviors* that are provoked by an emotion that are judged as good, bad, or neutral by their actual consequences. Although we can't take responsibility for our feelings, which just happen to us, we *can*—and must—take responsibility for our actions. We can't control how we feel, but we *can* control how we behave, as well as some of the circumstances that give rise to our feelings in the first place.

One important lesson often learned the hard way is think before you act. Here the message isn't to stop and think before *everything* you do, but to develop an approach to handling your emotions so that you don't act in haste or guided by emotions alone. In fact, the more intense the emotion, the more you should pay attention to it. People can get swept away by their feelings and act impulsively, only to later regret what they did. High emotions are not invitations to action; they're a statement that something powerful is happening to you, and a message to start thinking *before* acting.

The more intense the emotion, the more you should pay attention to it.

There's a subtle difference that distinguishes *impetuous* behavior from *spontaneous* behavior. We usually refer to someone who acts without thinking as impetuous or rash, whereas spontaneous decisions usually involve a conscious process, even if only momentary, before the action that follows. The former is a reaction, the latter a decision. Although not every emotion requires a thoughtful response, and not every behavior requires forethought, it is thinking that acts as a buffer between the two. Thought exists *between* emotions and behavior. Without thinking, we act blindly.

The Power of Self-Expression

One thing made possible by the power of thought is our ability to be expressive. What does self-expression mean, and how does it help? Job loss studies strongly suggest that people who write about their feelings and thoughts return to work more quickly than people who don't express themselves in this way. People who write about their feelings tend to return to work more quickly than people who write only about their concrete experiences and plans. In addition, people who write about their thoughts and feelings remain physically healthier than people who don't write during difficult times.

Emotions can create incredible pressure inside of you, building to boiling point. Many believe that the sort of stress associated with this internal pressure can eat away at you, contributing to physical illness such as migraine headaches, stomach problems, and heart attacks. It's common to hear people say they felt like they were going to explode, or talk about letting off steam. This release of emotional pressure is a form of expression; a release of something that was once held inside. Typically, though, self-expression is not simply a means of relieving pressure, but a means of transforming thoughts and feelings into action.

Self-expression is not simply a means of relieving pressure, but a means of transforming thoughts and feelings into action.

Self-expression allows wordless emotions to be expressed in ways that they can be seen and felt, through writing or art, for instance. Once expressed in this way, you can look at your thoughts and feelings and learn to use them as a tool for growth and the basis for careful decision making. Self-expression becomes a means for problem solving and decision making.

Self-expression not only transforms internal pressure, it transforms *you*. Talking about a problem situation doesn't change the situation, but it can help you to see things differently, to relieve the pressure of the situation, and to feel less emotionally entangled.

Self-Awareness

Part of managing feelings is self-expression. Before you can express a feeling, however, you have to recognize that you're having one so that you can then identify and understand it.

But the ability to recognize, identify, and understand your feelings doesn't eliminate them. Neither does self-expression. These are the steps to emotional regulation—the management of thoughts and feelings so they help your personal growth and aid you in achieving your goals.

Self-Defeating Cycles

Expression involves a form of action or the releasing of the emotion. No matter what you do, feelings don't just go away. Sometimes you simply have to be able to tolerate a bad feeling while it slowly fades over time or the situation changes. This may mean developing the skills to cope in the meantime so that your negative feelings don't roll you over.

Feelings can overcome you in a couple of ways, both of which inevitably lead to more problems. Some people will go to great lengths to try to get rid of their feelings: they'll drink heavily, use drugs, become abusive, overeat, or undereat. In short, they'll try to get rid of their feelings as quickly as they can by engaging in behaviors that are more reactions to feelings than solutions. These sorts of self-destructive or self-defeating behaviors often lead to still more problems, and the vicious cycle continues.

The first step in managing emotions is recognizing how you're feeling.

People can also develop a pattern of thinking that's quite negative and distorted if they can't cope with their feelings. For example, people may come to believe that they can *never* win or that things *never* turn out right for them. Distorted thoughts can include the idea that you're not good enough, that people are never going to give you a chance, or that you're just plain flawed and unlikable. These sorts of distortions become part of a pattern of irrational thoughts that in turn lead to still more negative feelings, which creates a negative cycle with a self-fulfilling prophecy of failure and hopelessness.

The first step in managing emotions is recognizing how you're feeling. Use the next entry any time you want to think about how you're feeling. You can also complete the entry shortly before or after a situation that may be emotional for you in some way or another or when you find feelings washing over you. It provides a simple way to help pick up and understand a feeling. As the entry can be used repeatedly, you may want to copy the blank entry before you complete it for the first time.

MY FEELINGS

I. Use this checklist of feelings to think about recent or current feelings and why you're feeling this way. Check all feelings that apply, and add additional feelings to the end of the list.

How I Feel   Why I Feel This Way

__abandoned _____

__afraid _____

__agitated _____

__angry _____

__anxious _____

__ashamed _____

__betrayed _____

__bitter _____

__detached _____

__disappointed _____

__foolish _____

__guilty _____

__happy _____

__helpless _____

__hopeful _____

__hopeless _____

__hurt _____

__ignored _____

___incapable _____

___irritated _____

___lonely _____

___loved _____

___numb _____

___overwhelmed _____

___regretful _____

___remorseful _____

___sad _____

___shocked _____

___sorrowful _____

___supported _____

___trapped _____

___vulnerable _____

___worried _____

___worthless _____

___yearning _____

other: _____ _____

_____ _____

_____ _____

2. Think about the feelings you've named and the source or reasons for each feeling. What do your feelings say about this time in your life?

_____

_____

_____

_____

_____

3. What do your feelings tell you about *yourself* at this time in your life?

_____

_____

_____

_____

The Immediacy of Feelings

Feelings and thoughts are quite different in that we can always write down our thoughts and come back to them later. You can switch gears with your thinking and continue that line of thought at a later time. But emotions are immediate. You feel them right now, and they're often not under your control. Although you may be able to cope with the feeling, you can't just wish it away or put it one side and return to it later. *Ignoring* an emotion means not allowing that emotion to direct or control your behavior at that moment. That way, you can continue what you're doing without being distracted by your underlying feeling. It doesn't mean switching the emotion off (even if you could), or pretending it's not there.

Of course, even though this is a difficult time in your life, not all your feelings are negative. There are times when things are upbeat and you feel good. It's important to recognize and think about these times. Use the next journal entry to think about your feelings *right now,* and consider using the entry each time you want to capture and reflect upon your emotions.

Ignoring an emotion means not allowing that emotion to direct or control your behavior at that moment.

HOW DO YOU FEEL RIGHT NOW?

1. What are you feeling right now?

_____

_____

_____

_____

_____

2. Describe your feelings in a single word. _____

3. Put this emotion into words.

a. *This feeling is . . .* _____

_____

b. *If this feeling had a color it would be . . .* _____

_____

c. *If this feeling had texture it would be . . .* _____

_____

d. *If this feeling made a noise it would sound like . . .* _____

_____

e. Put your emotion into words. *I feel . . .* _____

_____

_____

_____

_____

_____

_____

4. How long have you been feeling this way?

_____

_____

5. What led to this feeling?

_____

_____

_____

6. Is this a common emotion for you?

_____

_____

_____

7. What does this feeling tell you?

_____

_____

_____

_____

_____

THINGS TO THINK ABOUT

- If this is an unpleasant feeling, what can you do to avoid situations that lead to this feeling? If it's a pleasant feeling, what sort of situations or relationships stimulate this feeling and keep it alive?
- Have the types or frequency of your feelings changed over time? In what ways?
- Are your emotions so long-lasting or intense that they affect your ability to function? If they are, do you feel you need help coping with them?

Dealing with Feelings

Knowing that you have feelings and being able to identify them are important steps in managing your emotions. Still, knowing you're angry or sad doesn't necessarily mean you know how to tolerate or deal with the feeling.

Essentially, dealing with feelings comes down to four steps:

1. *Tolerate* the feeling. This involves accepting it, putting up with it, and finding a way to live with it no matter how unpleasant the feeling may be.

2. *Cope* with the pressure of the feeling. Find a way to ensure that the feeling doesn't push you into behavior that you know is bad for you, bad for others, or in some other way inappropriate.

3. *Listen* to the feeling. Understanding the meaning of the emotion involves listening to it: why you're feeling this way, what's causing the feeling, and what the feeling is telling you about the situation.

4. *Respond* to the feeling with an appropriate response. This may mean telling someone how you feel, taking a walk or being alone, sometimes crying and sometimes yelling, or not doing anything at all.

Dealing *with a feeling means that you've expressed that emotional pressure and can move on without being controlled by the emotion.*

Each one of these steps is important, and each leads to the next until the feeling has been dealt with and is no longer acting as a source of pressure. *Dealing* with a feeling means that you've expressed that emotional pressure and can move on without being controlled by the emotion. In the ideal emotional situation, dealing with a feeling involves all four of these steps, but each step is important in it's own right. Even if you never get to Step 2 in this sequence, tolerating the feeling has value too.

People usually don't have to deal with pleasant feelings. It's the unpleasant ones we have to cope with—sadness, bitterness, depression, anger, anxiety, shame, and guilt, to name but a few. These are feelings you're almost bound to experience during your lifetime, especially when things go wrong. The issues aren't about having these feelings, but about how you'll *deal* with them.

Use the next entry to deal with one feeling at a time. Repeat the entry to revisit the same feeling again, or use it to think about a different feeling.

ONE AT A TIME

1. Think about which six emotions are typically the most difficult for you to tolerate or manage.

_____   _____

_____   _____

_____   _____

2. Pick one of these emotions for this entry. _____

3. Describe how this emotion typically affects you.

_____

_____

_____

4. Why is this feeling so difficult to handle?

_____

_____

_____

5. How do you feel like *behaving* when you have this feeling?

_____

_____

_____

6. What should you *not* do when you're feeling this way, and why not?

_____

_____

_____

_____

7. What are the possible consequences if the way you behave in response to this feeling is inappropriate?

_____

_____

_____

_____

8. What are five ways you might be able to deal with this feeling? Use this checklist; then add your own ideas.

__cry   __do something physical   __do something social

__draw   __go running   __hit a punching bag

__play a sport   __read a book   __make or build something

__take a walk   __talk to a counselor   __talk to a friend

__write   __talk to my spouse   __yell into a pillow

other: _____   _____

_____   _____

_____   _____

9. What, if anything, keeps you from dealing with this feeling in a positive way?

_____

_____

_____

_____

- What will happen in the long run, if you *don't* learn to cope with this feeling?
- Are there many feelings that are difficult for you to deal with, or just one or two?
- In general, what helps the most in dealing with difficult feelings?

What You Do Is Who You Are: Coping Behaviors

Your behavior is what you do. It's what other people see or know about you. Behavior is the outward expression of what's going on inside of you. No one can see inside your mind or read your thoughts, but they can see how you deal with this inner experience. Behavior includes the things you actually *do,* like yell, cry, mope, get angry, or laugh, as well as the things you say. It also includes the things that people can observe about you, such as your attitude, body language, and how you spend your time. Behavior also includes the things you *don't* do, like not speaking or saying hello to someone, not attending a meeting, or not finishing something you started. In other words, your behaviors include almost every facet of your interactions with the world and the people in it. And, just as there's no such thing as nonaction, there's no such thing as nonbehavior.

Behavior is the outward expression of what's going on inside of you. No one can see inside your mind or read your thoughts, but they can see how you deal with this inner experience.

There are many kinds of behaviors that help us deal with feelings and situations. Coping behaviors are those things we do to help express and vent emotional pressure. Although some people engage in unhealthy behaviors, such as smoking or drinking heavily, isolating themselves or staying in bed all day, getting high, or becoming abusive to other people in an effort to cope with or forget their troubles, these really *aren't* coping behaviors, as they only increase problems. Negative coping behaviors are really *attempts* to cope that don't work. Coping behaviors *improve,* not worsen, your situation and strengthen your ability to deal with issues. Effective coping is always healthy, and means:

- knowing when you have feelings—being in touch with what's going on inside
- identifying feelings—recognizing and being able to name the feelings
- tolerating feelings—accepting the feelings and not trying to escape them
- managing feelings—controlling your feelings, not letting them control you
- understanding feelings— connecting your feelings to their causes
- expressing feelings—allowing your feelings to emerge and be expressed

Coping behaviors are those things we do to help express and vent emotional pressure. Coping behaviors improve, not worsen, your situation and strengthen your ability to deal with issues.

Focus the next entry on your coping behaviors. Your writing will help you to think about ways both to deal with your feelings and behaviors to *avoid* when you experience difficult emotions.

COPING BEHAVIORS

1. How do you deal with your feelings?

_____

_____

_____

_____

2. Can you tolerate difficult feelings? Give an example.

_____

_____

_____

_____

3. Do you give in to your feelings and act upon them without thinking? When has this happened?

_____

_____

_____

4. What's the healthiest way you deal with your feelings?

_____

_____

_____

5. Do you ever get caught in, or create, self-defeating cycles of behavior that hinder or hurt you instead of helping to appropriately express feelings? What are they?

_____

_____

_____

6. Which of your behaviors are the healthiest when it comes to dealing with your feelings?

_____

_____

_____

THINGS TO THINK ABOUT

- Was it difficult to look at your own behaviors? Did you learn anything about yourself? How are your emotions and your behaviors connected?
- Is your behavioral style helping, hindering, or hurting you? Are there behavioral patterns you need to think more about or change?
- Do you ever hide your behaviors from others? If you do, why?

Self-Defeating Thinking

The link between emotions and behavior is thought. But our thinking can sometimes be irrational and unclear. At these times, we interpret our experiences in a way that is neither helpful nor rational. People can have knee-jerk responses to situations when they don't allow their minds to intervene and sort through what's happening.

Many times this style of thinking and responding hampers the development of self-esteem because it becomes part of a negative cycle where a poor self-image is often built upon incorrect assumptions about yourself or other people. These assumptions can lead to a misinterpretation of the things that happen to you, which may trigger knee-jerk reactions and behaviors that can have unpleasant emotional or practical consequences. The consequences can lead back to the sense that nothing ever goes right for you, so low self-esteem is confirmed and a poor self-image is built.

Self-defeating cycles can only be interrupted by understanding how you respond to situations and learning how to change your *irrational* thoughts and beliefs to thoughts and beliefs that are more *rational* and *realistic*.

Complete the following journal entry for a quick exploration of the ways in which your thinking may be irrational or distorted at times. These sort of thinking patterns are sometimes known as *cognitive distortions*.

Self-defeating cycles can only be interrupted by understanding how you respond to situations and learning how to change your irrational thoughts and beliefs to thoughts and beliefs that are more rational and realistic.

DISTORTIONS IN THINKING

1. Briefly review each of these types of irrational thinking styles. Check off any that fit the way you think, either in general or during this time in your life.

__*Emotional misreasoning.* You draw an irrational and incorrect conclusion based on the way you feel at that moment. *I feel this way, therefore I am this way. I feel like a piece of garbage, so I must be a piece of garbage.*

__*Overgeneralization*. You reach an incorrect conclusion that has far-reaching implications based on a single experience or a small set of experiences. You assume that your experience in one situation is a reflection of the ways things are in *all* situations. *I failed to do well in* this *job, so I will fail in* all *jobs.*

__*Catastrophic thinking*. You magnify the impact of negative experiences to extreme proportions. *If I fail in* this *job, my entire career will fall to pieces.*

__*Black-and-white thinking*. You see things as all-or-nothing, where things are *either* one way *or* the other. Either *I'm a success in this job,* or *I'm a total failure.* If *I'm not perfect,* then *I must be imperfect.*

__*Shoulds and musts*. You feel you *should* do something or things *must* be a certain way. You feel that you absolutely *must* behave in a particular way or think that you *should* have a level of control over the world around you. *I should* have been more successful in *my job. I* must *succeed in this job.*

__*Negative predictions/Fortune-telling*. You predict failure in situations yet to happen because things have gone wrong before. *I didn't* do well in this job, and therefore I will never *do well in any job.*

__*Projection*. You make negative assumptions about the thoughts, intentions, or motives of another person that are often projections of your own thought and feelings about the situation. *He knows my job didn't work out. He thinks that it's my fault and that I'm a loser.*

__*Mind reading*. You feel that others should have known how you felt or what you wanted even though you didn't tell them. *She ought to know that I need to feel comforted even if I didn't tell her. He ought to know I need his support now.*

__*Labeling*. You label yourself or someone else in a negative way, which shapes and oversimplifies the way you see yourself or that other person. *Because this job has failed, I'm a failure. Because my boss fired me, he's no good at all.*

__*Personalization*. You treat a negative event as a personal reflection or confirmation of your own worthlessness. *Because I wound up losing my job, I'm a failure — as I knew anyway. Nothing ever goes right for me because I'm worthless.*

__*Negative focus.* You focus on negative events, memories, or implications while ignoring more neutral or positive information about yourself or a situation. *It doesn't matter that I have two children who care for and love me or that I have been successful in my marriage. I'm no good and a failure because my job didn't work out as planned.*

__*Cognitive avoidance.* You avoid thinking about emotionally difficult subjects because they feel overwhelming or insurmountable. *I can't even think about it, let alone try to understand and change it.*

2. Are there are other types of cognitive distortions that characterize your thinking at times? What are they?

_____

_____

_____

_____

_____

3. Are these sort of cognitive distortions affecting your self-esteem and self-image? Explain.

_____

_____

_____

_____

_____

THINGS TO THINK ABOUT

- How can you tell when your thinking is distorted or irrational?
- How might distortions in your thinking, if not corrected, affect the course of finding a new job?
- Can you think of recent situations in which you applied cognitively distorted thinking?

A Daily Journal

Writing helps—even a few words each day can help unload thoughts and feelings and help put your day into perspective. This whole chapter has been about regulating and managing your feelings by putting them out there where you see them, think about them, and use them to help guide your way. The next section provides a format for a daily journal entry. This is a simple entry that you can use to unload your thoughts and feelings, describe your day, and record what you're going through as part of your personal history. If you decide to use this format daily, make sure you copy the blank before using it for the first time.

At the end of the entry add a thought for the day. This can be anything that impresses, inspires, or strikes you as being in some way worth remembering. Finding a thought for each day pushes you to look outside of yourself, even as you find ways to express what's inside.

A DAILY DIARY

Day: _____ Date: _____

1. What were the most pressing issues on your mind today?

_____

_____

_____

_____

2. What special tasks, events, or incidents stand out?

_____

_____

_____

_____

3. What did you accomplish today?

_____

_____

_____

_____

_____

4. In general, how were you affected by this day?

_____

_____

_____

_____

_____

5. What's changing over time? Are the days getting easier or harder? Are you more hopeful or less hopeful? Are issues getting resolved or building up?

_____

_____

_____

_____

6. What's going right?

_____

_____

_____

_____

_____

7. Today I'm feeling . . .

_____

_____

_____

_____

8. I want/need to say . . .

_____

_____

_____

_____

9. Other reflections on the day or this time in your life:

_____

_____

_____

_____

_____

_____

_____

Thought for the day:

_____

_____

_____

_____

_____

Checkpoint: Dealing with Feelings

As you wrap up your work in this chapter, remember that you're not alone in your life. You have friends and family, and they're both supporters for you and affected by you.

At this time in your life, when you're experiencing many difficult moments, feelings, and moods, it's easy to displace your feelings onto someone or something else. Displacement is easiest to do when you're not conscious of doing it, and it begins when you're not even aware you're having a feeling or you're trying to pretend the feeling is not there. Even if you don't recognize the feeling, or are ignoring it, it doesn't go away. Instead, the feeling may get expressed, usually inappropriately, through displacement. You let off steam in the wrong way and probably at the wrong person.

Displacing your feelings onto others—dumping—is not fair to them and keeps you from dealing directly with the real source of your feelings.

It's better to express your feelings directly: cry, yell, say how angry, sad, or scared you are without losing sight of exactly what it *is* you're sad, upset, or frightened about. Displacing your feelings onto others—dumping—is not fair to them and keeps you from dealing directly with the real source of your feelings.

As you complete the work in this chapter, it's important that you're in touch with your feelings and how you express them. Feelings are like weathervanes. They don't explain the weather, but they show you the direction and intensity of the wind. Feelings are the weathervane to your emotions—they don't necessarily offer insight into *why* you might be feeling emotional, but they are the direct line inside. If you stay in touch with your feelings, you'll have an important gauge of your emotional health, which can help you control your emotions rather than letting your emotions control you.

8

Destination:
MANAGING PRACTICAL MATTERS

RAY

I lost my job as regional manager when the firm closed that office. Losing my job was bad enough, but worse times were to follow. We'd built a new home and two weeks after I learned about the closing we moved into it. We were approved for the construction loan months before, and our whole budget had been based on my management salary. Now I had no salary at all.

For the next six months we lived on the edge. My wife worked and I was getting unemployment, and we were just getting by. At first I refused to acknowledge that we were now living well beyond our means and wouldn't consider the idea of selling the house we'd just built, even though living there was killing us. I also wouldn't consider settling for a job with lower pay and lower rank, and kept hoping that something would come along and I'd be earning a decent salary again. Well, that never happened, or at least not the way I wanted it to. We made the decision to stay in the house and live the life we wanted, but we also agreed to pay the price for that decision. We canceled the vacation we'd planned and cut back on other things that were now luxuries. We made and lived by a budget

129

and figured out our expenses and income almost to the penny. I took a job that I really didn't want and that paid less than I needed, and I wound up working a second job as well.

That got us through this very rough patch, and eventually I managed to get back on my feet and into a work situation I felt okay about. It took almost two years before I could say we fully recovered from the job loss, but we got through it because we were willing to face the realities and make some difficult choices about what we most wanted and how to best manage.

The ability to sustain yourself and survive during this difficult period involves many factors.

ONE OF THE first and most immediate concerns faced by many people when they lose their jobs is financial, but practical matters involve more than just financial consideration. These include the practical tasks of looking for a new job, getting help with child care and other daily matters, maintaining an appropriate lifestyle, and taking care of emotional and physical health. Although money helps build a life free of financial stress and emotional worry, many other things also affect the quality of life, and there's more to survival than money alone.

The ability to sustain yourself and survive during this difficult period involves many factors. Some of these, such as emotional balance, maintaining self-esteem, and personal support, have already been covered in previous chapters. Others, such as network development and planning skills, are covered in later chapters. In many ways this current chapter is a watershed chapter, the turning point that brings together the work you've done and sets the pace for the work ahead.

This chapter will help you to recognize your most pressing practical needs and think about how to sustain yourself and weather this storm. It's important to recognize that financial realities are key for most. Without basic financial stability it will be difficult to build a solid base upon which to plan and build your future. However, the goal of this chapter is not to resolve basic financial issues. There are many resources available to help you resolve financial problems, build personal budgets, develop effective habits, and design and pursue job searches. By the end of this chapter you will have a clearer sense of the sort of assistance you may need and where to find it.

Determinants of Practical Difficulties

People face many practical difficulties that go beyond just money. In fact, the practical difficulties are usually the things that interfere with picking up and getting on with life. The sort of practical issues you face will be determined by a number of factors —some within your control and some outside of your direct influence.

First, what *is* practical reality? If you've already worked your way through Chapter 3 ("Destination: Dealing with Reality"), you're aware that the reality of your life is somewhat shaped by your expectations and the way you define your life. But *practical* reality generally includes the daily *tasks* of managing your life, like paying bills, taking care of the kids, finding job leads, generating a resume, and getting yourself into the job market. Another aspect of practical reality is the *ability* to take care of these daily, and often tedious, tasks. This means staying emotionally and physically healthy so you can function well enough to accomplish practical tasks.

There are many variables that affect the practical reality of each individual. Broadly, these factors include the following.

* *Personality factors.* These involve who you are as a person. Are you able to recognize your needs and, if you are, can you ask for help? Are you a "loner" who neither needs nor seeks support, or are you someone who requires and seeks out emotional and spiritual ties to others? Personality is certainly a factor in recognizing needs and accepting help;

There are many resources available to help you resolve financial problems, build personal budgets, develop effective habits, and design and pursue job searches.

people who have a difficult time in either area may find it especially difficult to get their practical needs met.

Practical reality includes the daily tasks of managing your life, like paying bills, taking care of the kids, find job leads, generating a resume, and getting yourself into the job market.

◆ *Gender.* Although stereotypes about men and women are changing, it's still true that men in our culture are often expected to "take it on the chin" without complaining, or at least without telling anybody else how they may *really* feel. Some men may have a difficult time accurately recognizing their feelings or asking for help. Conversely, women in our society are often far more adept at expressing and sharing their feelings and getting emotional support. Their need for emotional and practical support may also be more visible to others, so help may come without even having to ask for it. Gender isn't something you have any control over, but you should certainly recognize it as a variable as you start thinking about the practical realities of your life.

◆ *Age and time on previous job.* People approaching middle age or beyond, and especially those who have been in one or two jobs most of their adult lives, are likely to face more challenges and need more help than their younger counterparts. Here, the issues may clearly overlap with gender issues. It can be difficult to find work as you age, and it can be emotionally difficult to even *think* about a new job when you were in your last job for twenty years.

◆ *Daily needs.* The kind of help needed is clearly going to depend to a great degree on your day-to-day reality. If you're a single parent, for instance, and have suddenly lost your source of income and have to find a job, you're bound to need practical help in the simple management of daily life.

◆ *Financial problems.* Many people face severe financial difficulties after being out of work for any length of time. These include paying routine bills as well as the costs of finding a new job or retraining. People who have no savings and who are just managing to cover their costs when they're working are going to face additional emotional stress and financial hardship. This is often the area of most immediate concern following job loss.

- *Mental and physical health.* For some people, the emotional issues, financial strains, or other difficulties created by job loss are too difficult to deal with alone. They lead to minor or major mental health issues, which range from the need to seek direction and counseling from a therapist or support group to episodes of severe depression or anxiety. Mental health issues are often related to strains on physical health as well.

There are many other factors at play in determining practical reality for you, and it is the interplay of these factors (as well as your own expectations) that shapes your particular reality.

There are, of course, many other factors at play in determining practical reality for you, and it is the interplay of these factors (as well as your own expectations) that shapes your particular reality. It's important to recognize that some factors are within your direct control, while others aren't. It's equally important to be able to distinguish between the two.

Attitude is everything. It's probably the one thing that we have the most control over, although it may sometimes seem impossible to change. Use this next journal entry to reflect upon a simple verse that offers a basic formula for managing practical reality.

WISDOM

"Grant me the serenity to accept the things I cannot change, courage to change the things I can, and wisdom to know the difference."
— REINHOLD NIEBUHR

1. Briefly reflect on the verse above. What does it mean to you?

_____

_____

_____

_____

2. What can you learn from this verse?

_____

_____

_____

_____

3. Does "acceptance" mean giving in? Can you overcome even those things you must accept?

_____

_____

_____

4. What does "courage" mean to you when it comes to personal change?

_____

_____

_____

5. What does it mean to be "serene" during this time in your life?

_____

_____

_____

6. List up to ten practical needs in your life right now. Next to each, check off whether you have control over getting this need met, and then briefly explain your answer.

Practical Need	Control/No Control	Because
_____	____ ____	_____
_____	____ ____	_____
_____	____ ____	_____
_____	____ ____	_____
_____	____ ____	_____

Practical Need	Control/No Control		Because
_____	____	____	_____
_____	____	____	_____
_____	____	____	_____
_____	____	____	_____
_____	____	____	_____

7. How can you take control over even the uncontrollable things in your life?

_____

_____

_____

_____

_____

THINGS TO THINK ABOUT

- What will most help you to overcome difficulties at this time in your life? Can your attitude help bring about change?
- In what ways are you responsible for creating an environment in which change can happen? What most gets in the way of building that environment?
- Is it important to find serenity in your life right now? What do you need to do to build or find serenity?

Assessing Your Needs

Stabilizing means taking control over the immediate financial, emotional, and other problems that are dominating your everyday life.

What factors are influencing or determining your immediate situation? Stabilizing means taking control over the immediate financial, emotional, and other problems that are dominating your everyday life. Your success in dealing with the tasks and issues of future stages will be built upon your ability to deal with the practical issues facing you today.

Given the critical nature of managing your life right now and coping with the many issues you may be facing, it's important to think about and understand how you're doing and where you may need help.

PRACTICAL REALITIES

1. Are you satisfied with how you're dealing with practical tasks? Why or why not?

_____

_____

_____

_____

2. In what ways are you having the most difficulty dealing with practical matters?

_____

_____

_____

_____

3. What adjustments must you make in order to better deal with practical reality?

_____

_____

_____

_____

4. What sort of factors are affecting your ability to manage your daily life or the practical responsibilities you have? Check off any that apply, and add others that apply.

___*Personality factors.* Is there something about the sort of person you are and the way you deal with things that's affecting the way you're managing tasks?

___*Gender.* Is your gender affecting your ability to handle some, or all, of the practical tasks you're facing?

___*Age.* Is your age creating problems for you in dealing with daily tasks and practical reality?

___*Length of time in previous job.* Is the amount of time on your last job affecting your ability to seek out new work?

___*Daily needs.* Are the amount or types of daily practical tasks just too much for you to handle alone?

___*Financial problems.* Are money matters significantly affecting your ability to manage your life?

___*Mental and physical health.* Are you facing a depression, anxiety, or other mood problem that is affecting your ability to function in your daily life? Is your physical health a problem in some way? Are you developing a problem with alcohol, drugs, eating, or other behaviors that are interfering with daily tasks and life responsibilities?

other: _____

_____

_____

5. In what ways are the factors you checked off affecting your ability to manage daily and practical activities?

_____

_____

_____

_____

_____

6. In what ways can you begin to exert some control over the things that influence your practical needs?

_____

_____

_____

_____

7. Do you need help? Look back at your journal entries in Chapter 6 ("Destination: Support"). Based on what you're thinking and writing about now, do those entries accurately represent or reflect the kind of help you need or are getting?

_____

_____

_____

_____

8. What sort of help is most needed?

_____

_____

_____

_____

9. In Chapter 6 you wrote about natural and drafted support. Do you need to look for more help in managing practical tasks within your natural support system, or do you need to seek out more drafted support? How can you get help from these support systems?

_____

_____

_____

_____

_____

Practical Plans

Practical needs call for practical plans. These fall into two categories. Plans with *tangible* outcomes lead to results that you can directly see. Tangible outcomes involve things like reducing expenses or increasing income, getting help with child care, improving physical health, developing concrete job leads and interviews, and, of course, finding a job.

Plans with *intangible* outcomes involve positive changes in attitude, mental health, personal learning, and self-esteem. Although these are not outcomes that can be directly seen, they're as important as tangible goals and contribute to or are responsible for those tangible outcomes. Regardless of whether intangible outcomes are directly observable or not, the action plan to accomplish those goals involves steps that are quite concrete.

Although these sort of steps are often connected to tangible outcomes, concrete steps can also lead to intangible outcomes. For instance, your very use of this journal is a *tangible* step to bring about the *intangible* goal of personal growth and improved self-esteem. In other words, personal goals that are not easily measured—things like changes in attitude, beliefs, or values or improved mental health—can be achieved through very concrete steps. You can improve your mental health through the

Plans with tangible *outcomes lead to results that you can directly see. Plans with* intangible *outcomes involve positive changes in attitude, mental health, personal learning, and self-esteem.*

Personal goals that are not easily measured—things like changes in attitude, beliefs, or values or improved mental health—can be achieved through very concrete steps.

concrete steps of seeing a counselor or build your sense of support and connection by joining or forming a mutual support group. You can get help assessing and managing your financial matters by working with an accountant, banker, or financial advisor. You can improve the quality of your life by planning to spend more time with family or friends, or by spending a certain number of hours each week involved in a sport or something else that enhances your sense of well-being.

People often limit themselves in taking care of their own practical needs. They feel they don't have the skills, lack the imagination to find solutions, or need to be rescued. They fear failure, lack the energy, are overwhelmed with difficult emotions, are abusing alcohol or drugs and so are incapacitated, or are feeling very sorry for themselves. In this way, people not only fail to get their needs met, but they become their own worst enemy as well. This is another one of those self-defeating cycles.

Sometimes it's important to tilt your head to one side to see things a little differently so you can realize solutions. Use the next journal entry to think generally about practical matters in your life right now and how you're managing them.

PLANNING FOR YOUR LIFE

1. Check off all areas that have to be managed in your current daily life, and add others that are currently relevant.

__building a job network

__improving financial situation

__improving personal attitude

__improving relationships

__improving support

__getting help managing daily life

__improving mental health

__improving physical health

__improving self-esteem

__improving the way you think

___ improving use of available time   ___ planning a job search

___ using supportive relationships   ___ using time more productively

other: _____   _____

_____   _____

2. What most gets in the way of dealing with practical matters?

_____

_____

_____

_____

3. List five reasons why you *can't* have what you want or get your needs met. *I can't get my needs met or manage my daily life because . . .*

a. _____

b. _____

c. _____

d. _____

e. _____

4. Myths are popular legends, sometimes based on a grain of truth, but often created to explain something away. Myths become ingrained in our history and sometimes prevent growth if not explored and dispelled. Briefly restate each of your answers to Question 3, and then dispel each explanation of why you can't get your needs met.

I can't get my needs met because . . .   *This is a myth because . . .*

a. _____   _____

b. _____   _____

c. _____   _____

d. _____   _____

e. _____   _____

5. Are you a good friend to yourself, your own worst enemy, or something in between?

_____

_____

_____

6. What personal obstacles do you have to overcome in order to effectively manage your daily needs?

_____

_____

_____

_____

7. What's the most difficult thing to contemplate as you consider how to best manage current needs? Why?

_____

_____

_____

_____

THINGS TO THINK ABOUT

- Is it difficult to think about turning to others for help? If it is, why?
- What personal changes do you need to make to ensure that you're able to manage daily needs and build a base for future success?
- If married, are you including your spouse in your decision making and plans? If you have children, are you allowing them to be part of the solution?

Action Steps

Figuring out a solution doesn't have to involve a detailed plan, but having a clear plan provides a way to think through and map out a solution. An action plan of any kind is built on least three things.

- *Understanding the problem.* This is more than simply knowing you have a problem you want to correct. It means having a sense of the *cause* of the problem. Although job loss is the obvious cause of problems in this case, the fact that someone has no savings, few marketable job skills, or poor support may actually be the more significant underlying cause of the immediate problem.

- *A goal.* What do you actually want to accomplish? How will you know you've fixed the problem or met the need?

- *Action steps.* What are you going to *do* to address the situation? A goal of managing a household budget, for instance, might include steps like listing household expenses, separating essential from nonessential expenses (like groceries versus dining out, utilities versus cable televison, job-hunting travel expenses versus vacations), evaluating current sources of income (spouse salary, dividends and interest, pension, and so forth), considering loans and sources of loans, and discussing possible solutions with other family members. A second set of steps involved in this same scenario will involve implementing your new budget and ongoing discussion with other family members who may be affected by the changes. Other goals will involve other steps, of course, but the basic idea is that there are clear things you have to do to get your plan off the drawing board and into action.

As you think about putting the steps into action, it will be important to consider what sort of help you can draw on, what re-

As you think about putting the steps into action, it will be important to consider what sort of help you can draw on, what resources are available, what obstacles must be overcome, and what alternatives can you fall back on, if necessary.

sources are available, what obstacles must be overcome, and what alternatives can you fall back on, if necessary.

Although a detailed action plan is beyond the scope of this book, you can use your journal to think about and outline steps. There are any number of resources available to you for a more thorough development of these ideas and steps, including financial- and career-planning workbooks, motivational tapes and videos, and listings of local resources. Check your local library for these materials and more. There's also professional help available to assist with almost any area of your life, including financial counseling, career development, relationships, and mental health. Don't forget the Internet, which has become a tremendous resource for ideas, reference materials, and people.

Use the next journal entry to outline an action plan for one area of your life that requires practical management right now. Copy the blank format before using it, and use it any time you need to think about different areas of your life that require practical management.

ACTION PLAN

1. Which area of your life requires an action plan for management?

_____

_____

2. Describe your concern.

_____

_____

_____

_____

_____

3. Besides your job loss itself, are there other underlying or related problems connected to this practical need?

_____

_____

_____

_____

_____

_____

4. What's your goal? What do you want to accomplish in managing this area?

_____

_____

_____

_____

_____

_____

5. What sort of action plan do you need to develop?

__build self-esteem and confidence   __build support

__design a plan to improve my health   __develop a household budget

__improve my mental health   __improve relationships

__research job opportunities/connections   __reduce expenses

__research job or career retraining   __write a financial plan

other: _____   _____

_____   _____

_____   _____

6. Outline the steps that are required to complete this goal. On each line, jot down individual steps that are required. Don't worry about their order. Once you've written

up to eight steps, go back and rank each step in the sequence you'll need to follow as you begin to implement the plan.

Description of the Action Step to Be Taken   Rank

_____   _____

_____   _____

_____   _____

_____   _____

_____   _____

_____   _____

_____   _____

_____   _____

7. What help, support, or resources will you need to accomplish your goal?

a. People in your natural support system (see Chapter 6):

_____

b. Drafted or professional help (see Chapter 6):

_____

c. Materials (books, videos, tapes, worksheets):

_____

d. Other:

_____

_____

8. What obstacles will you face in implementing your action steps?

_____

_____

_____

_____

9. Will you actually implement this action plan? If not, why not? If you will, how and when?

_____

_____

_____

_____

_____

THINGS TO THINK ABOUT

- Look back at your plan—is it realistic? Did you put enough thought into it? Do you need to go back and redo it?
- Is it useful to have an action plan? If so, why? If not, why not?
- If married, are you consulting with your spouse? If you have children, are you giving them a chance to be involved? If not, why not?

Big Decisions

After losing a job, people are often faced with huge life decisions. Many of these revolve around financial considerations, as well as locating new and satisfying work. However, the goal for now is _managing_ current practical matters, not _making_ big decisions or enormous changes.

Checkpoint: Managing Practical Matters

By now you know that some of the realities in your life are outside of your direct control. These must be tolerated and managed carefully as you work toward the future. Other practical matters, however, are within your control. These are the things that, in some way, are of your own making. As you near the end of this chapter, you're recognizing the difference between these two faces of your everyday life.

Use this final entry to think about what you're learning as you work your way through this difficult journey.

MANAGING YOURSELF

1. What have you learned that can help you better manage your life?

a. About yourself: _____

_____

b. About others: _____

_____

c. About support: _____

_____

d. About your family: _____

_____

e. About your friends: _____

_____

f. About the world: _____

_____

2. What have you learned about your capacity to adapt? How is your self-esteem now?

_____

_____

_____

_____

3. How much tougher are you now than you were when you began this journey?

_____

_____

_____

_____

4. In what ways is this period of your life a rite of passage?

_____

_____

_____

_____

5. What's different about the way you think now?

_____

_____

_____

_____

THINGS TO THINK ABOUT

- Are you sharing your experiences with other people? Are there other people you'd like to be sharing your experiences with?
- Are you involving other people who ought to be involved? Are you including your spouse and children in this journey? Are you including your friends?
- Is your journaling helping you to make sense of your experiences along the way or to relieve powerful feelings? What's the most useful aspect of journaling, and what's the least useful part?

9

Destination:

LOOKING BACK

YVONNE

After I was fired, I found myself looking back to better days. These weren't just the days I was employed, but times when I felt happier and life was much simpler. After many frustrating weeks looking for work and getting nowhere, I started to think a little differently about my past.

Slowly it dawned on me that I was in this spot because of my past, not in spite of it. Life seemed easier and less stressful in the past, but as I thought back I remembered that life really hadn't been so simple, and I started having some real regrets about choices I'd made, and choices I hadn't made. I began to realize that I was the product of my history, and not just a victim of lousy circumstances. From here, it became clear to me that I'd better start thinking about the past in a different way so that I could learn from it and get my present and my future into better shape.

Instead of just thinking back about how great things were and how much fun I had when I was young, I see my past now as my instructor. With a clearer backward vision, I find I have a clearer view of my future.

WHAT DO YOU see when you look back? What do you remember, and what do you feel? There are many who look back at the past with regret, or whose recollections are sad or disturbing. Some people see the past as their best days, when things were so much better or somehow more full of life. Others have fond recollections of their past, but still live happily in the present.

Some people feel like victims of their past. They see present problems and difficulties as a consequence of something that happened in the past, or they may feel that the same bad things keep happening over and over, as though they are trapped in limbo. Others don't think much about the past at all, or where they've come from. They never consider the impact, good or bad, on who they are today. In both of these cases, it's difficult to tap into the past and use it as a storehouse of important experiences and information, or as a stepping stone to the future. But it is. The past is prologue and in many ways sets the stage for the person you are today. The past is also instructional and provides you with the skills and experiences to make choices, build change, deal with issues, and decide who you want to be today. Without looking at your past, it's difficult to really understand who you are today, and even more difficult to draw a picture of the future.

In this chapter, journal entries will focus on your past—as a person, as an employee, and as a traveler. How do you see your past? How can you best use it now?

> *The past is prologue and in many ways sets the stage for the person you are today. The past is also instructional and provides you with the skills and experiences to make choices, build change, deal with issues, and decide who you want to be today.*

I AM WHAT I AM

1. *The past set the stage for my present life by* . . . _____

_____

_____

_____

2. *The past provided me with* . . . _____

_____

_____

_____

3. *The past has robbed me of* . . . _____

_____

_____

_____

4. *When I think of my past, I feel* . . . _____

_____

_____

_____

5. *About myself, my past has taught me* . . . _____

_____

_____

_____

6. What have you learned from your past?

_____

_____

_____

7. How have you benefited from your past?

_____

_____

_____

_____

Markers and Milestones

Some moments in your past are far more memorable than others, and some are far more influential. Some of these become markers in your life, signifying or highlighting important changes, or milestones that tell you how far you've come or how far you have to go.

Sometimes these landmarks are people or events or things that happened to you. Relationships often stand as markers or milestones, such as a first romance, a marriage, or an important friendship. Sometimes it's the person more than the relationship that counts; perhaps a parent or an uncle or aunt, a high school teacher, or a teammate. Other markers or milestones are things, like graduating junior high, winning a competition, going on to college, or leaving home. Perhaps your first job was a milestone.

There will continue to be markers and milestones in your life. Losing your job may itself have become an important marker of some kind or may yet prove to be a landmark. It has already become part of your history. There's a difference between your *past* and your *history.* The past is a record of what's happened, but history rises from the past and is separated and distinguished from everything else in it.

Your history involves those formative moments and events that stand out, from which your character is built, shaped, or af-

The past is a record of what's happened, but history rises from the past and is separated and distinguished from everything else in it.

fected. In order to make use of our history, we have to first remember it. Our history is sometimes hidden from us and we have to search it out.

In the next journal entry, think back to important landmarks in your history—the things that contributed to who you are today, or seemed to point the way. Landmarks can reside in your deep memory, dating back to early childhood, or they can be as recent as yesterday. It's not *when* they happened, but the impact on your life. Although the entry begins with a series of people, relationships, and events, it focuses on one landmark only, so you may want to photocopy it for future use.

LANDMARKS

1. Name five important people in your life.

Person	Your Age When You Met	His or Her Importance
_____	____	_____
_____	____	_____
_____	____	_____
_____	____	_____
_____	____	_____

2. Name five important relationships.

Relationship	Your Age When It Began	Significance
_____	____	_____
_____	____	_____
_____	____	_____
_____	____	_____
_____	____	_____

3. Name five important events.

Event	Your Age When It Occurred	Importance
_____	_____	_____
_____	_____	_____
_____	_____	_____
_____	_____	_____
_____	_____	_____

4. Pick one of these people, relationships, or events to focus on for the rest of the entry. _____

5. Some events or people in your life are "markers," reminding you of important changes or moments. Others are "milestones" that tell you how far you've come or how far you have to go. Is the landmark you've picked for this entry more like a marker or a milestone? Why?

_____

_____

_____

6. How was this a shaping or important landmark?

_____

_____

_____

_____

7. Looking back, how have you changed? Have you changed?

_____

_____

_____

_____

Biography of Your Career

Losing a job can be a blow for many reasons. It can feel like being thrown right out of the ring, away from the main event. If your job was a career, you may be feeling removed from an important part of your life and worried that you won't be able to get back in the game. For you, this job may have been part of a career that evolved over many years or took many steps to reach. Alternatively, your job may have been just one among many held over the years, and it may have been significant for other reasons.

Given the power of a career to influence and mold, it's no wonder that job *loss* can have a powerful effect. Without a job to shape your life right now, this is a good time to relax and think about *how* your jobs have shaped you. Look back and draw material from your own history that can help you to understand more about what you need from work and how you want to begin to move on with your life.

BIOGRAPHY OF A CAREER

1. List every job you've ever held, from your first to your most recent. Include every job for which you were paid, including your paper route or baby-sitting. There's room for twenty jobs here. If you need more space, continue your list on a separate piece of paper.

Job	Age	Job	Age
_____	___	_____	___
_____	___	_____	___
_____	___	_____	___
_____	___	_____	___
_____	___	_____	___
_____	___	_____	___
_____	___	_____	___
_____	___	_____	___
_____	___	_____	___
_____	___	_____	___

2. Are there any trends in your work history? Have you had a lot of jobs or only one or two? Have your jobs been similar, or have you changed careers a lot?

_____

_____

_____

_____

_____

_____

_____

_____

3. Pick the first "serious" job you held—that is, the first job that held any importance for you.

Job _____ Age _____ Years in job _____

What was going on in your life when you started this job? _____

_____

_____

_____

What was the importance of this job? _____

_____

_____

_____

Looking back, what did this job teach you about yourself? _____

_____

_____

_____

4. Thinking about all of the jobs you've held, whether three jobs or forty, pick an important job somewhere in the middle of your work career.

Job _____ Age _____ Years in job _____

What was going on in your life when you started this job? _____

_____

_____

_____

What was the importance of the job? _____

_____

_____

_____

Looking back, what did this job teach you about yourself? _____

_____

_____

_____

5. Now write about your most recent job—the one from which you were dismissed.

Job _____ Age _____ Years in job _____

What was going on in your life when you started this job? _____

_____

_____

_____

_____

Was this job important? _____

_____

_____

_____

_____

What did this job teach you about yourself? _____

_____

_____

_____

_____

6. Have there been other important jobs in your history? If so, pick one and briefly write about it now.

_____

_____

_____

_____

7. What can you learn about yourself from your history of jobs?

_____

_____

_____

_____

_____

8. How has your work life, and the jobs you've held, shaped and influenced the person you are today?

_____

_____

_____

_____

_____

9. Do you feel like a richer and more interesting person today because of your work history? If so, why? If not, why not?

_____

_____

_____

_____

_____

THINGS TO THINK ABOUT

- What has the relationship been between you and your work? What is it like to be without that relationship now?
- Over the course of your working life, what's changed the most in your attitude toward work and what work means to you?
- What's been the most positive aspect of your working life? What's been the least positive?

Expectations

No matter how much we might want to put certain things from our past behind us, things that once mattered can be influential throughout our lives. For instance, it can be difficult to shake off early feelings of insecurity, even in adulthood. Developmental issues in late childhood and adolescence often shape our relationships, interactions with others, and self-image for the rest of our lives.

Developmental issues in late childhood and adolescence often shape our relationships, interactions with others, and self-image for the rest of our lives.

People grow up under all sorts of pressures, both from within and from others. Often these pressures take the form of expectations about who you *should* be, what you *should* do, and what you *should* be able to do. At a time in your life when you've lost your job, you may feel as though you've failed to accomplish those things that were *expected* of you. Use this next journal entry to think about the expectations of others and your expectations of yourself, concentrating on how they've affected your self-esteem, self-image, and personal identity.

FAMILY EXPECTATIONS

1. What expectations did you have for yourself when you were still in high school?

_____

_____

_____

_____

2. What sort of expectations have others held of you?

a. Your parents

_____

_____

b. Your siblings or other important family members

_____

_____

c. If married or in a committed relationship, your partner

_____

_____

d. If you're a parent, your children

_____

_____

e. Other important people in your life

_____

_____

3. What are your expectations of yourself today?

_____

_____

_____

_____

4. How have the expectations of others shaped your choices?

_____

_____

_____

_____

5. How have you lived up to the expectations of others?

_____

_____

_____

_____

6. How have you failed to live up to the expectations of others?

_____

_____

_____

_____

7. What did you want to be?

_____

_____

_____

_____

_____

8. How did you get here?

_____

_____

_____

_____

_____

_____

THINGS TO THINK ABOUT

- Do you worry that you've let others down, or failed to meet their expectations of you? If you do, how can you best resolve this?
- Have the expectations of others been good for you, or a weight holding you down? Should you now free yourself of the expectations of others?
- Is it liberating to realize the impact that expectations have had upon your choices and your self-image, or is it depressing in some way?

The Past as Prologue

Some aspects of your past reside not only in your mind, but in things that capture and remind you of your history. Take a look into your past. Spend an evening looking at old photos, slides, videotapes, or home movies of yourself and your family. If you're a keeper of old letters, written by you or received from others, or if you kept diaries back then, pull them out and read back through them. If you have other memorabilia, such as awards, trophies, or mementos, take a tour of them. If you're married or in a committed relationship, sift through these memories with your partner.

As you look back, think about what you can learn about your life from these things, and think about how much it's changed. What were you doing for work, and how did work fit into your life back then? How have you changed? If you have a family, how has it changed? What things were important to you? Are they still?

When you've completed this look back into your past, think about how it's affected your thinking about the present and the future. Then complete the next entry, using it to describe your thoughts and reflect on the experience.

A LOOK BACK

1. What was striking about this experience of looking back into your past?

_____

_____

_____

_____

_____

2. What's no longer important that once was?

_____

_____

_____

_____

3. What's important now that never used to be?

_____

_____

_____

_____

4. What was important then that still is?

_____

_____

_____

_____

5. What have you gained over these years?

_____

_____

_____

_____

6. What do you miss most?

_____

_____

_____

_____

7. What have you learned from your look back?

_____

_____

_____

_____

_____

_____

_____

_____

_____

_____

_____

_____

THINGS TO THINK ABOUT

- Is it important to look back into history to better understand your present and how you got here?
- As you think about your life now compared to your life as it was, ask yourself if this is the way you want it to be. Does it have to be this way?
- If you shared this history with your spouse, what sort of extra dimension was added?

Drawing from the Past

Revisiting the past is often an important experience for many reasons: for nostalgia, to work things out, or to complete unfinished business. Journals are not only great places to record your current life and your march into the future, but they also provide a wonderful way to think back on your life and consider the relevance of what *was* to what *is*. If looking back at your past has been useful in making sense of your present, you may want to continue this backward glance.

The journal entries in this chapter have provided specific ways to focus your thinking on your history, but there are dozens of ways to look back and write about the past. These include repeating or modifying the structured journal entries provided in this chapter or simply writing about specific incidents, experiences, or people that stand out as important. Wrap up your work in this chapter with this final entry.

THEN AND NOW

1. Think back to when you still had your job. If you'd been asked to choose twelve nouns or adjectives to describe yourself at that time in your life, what would they be?

_____   _____

_____   _____

_____   _____

_____   _____

_____   _____

_____   _____

2. If you'd been asked to pick the four most important descriptors from the list, which ones would you have chosen and why?

Descriptor   Because

_____   _____

_____   _____

_____   _____

_____   _____

3. Now choose twelve nouns or adjectives that describe you now, during this time of change and adjustment.

_____   _____

_____   _____

_____   _____

_____   _____

_____   _____

_____   _____

4. Which four are the most important now and why?

           Descriptor   Because

_____   _____

_____   _____

_____   _____

_____   _____

5. How has job loss affected your list? If it has, why and how? If not, why not?

_____

_____

_____

_____

6. What do these two lists tell you about yourself?

_____

_____

_____

_____

7. What do these lists tell you about your adjustment?

_____

_____

_____

_____

8. Complete each of the following five sentences.

I used to be . . . _____, *but now I'm* . . . _____

I used to be . . . _____, *but now I'm* . . . _____

I used to be . . . _____, *but now I'm* . . . _____

I used to be . . . _____, *but now I'm* . . . _____

I used to be . . . _____, *but now I'm* . . . _____

THINGS TO THINK ABOUT

- Do you see your past as an ally or something to avoid? Either way, how can you best use your history to guide and shape your present and future decisions?
- As you complete this chapter, do you feel you have a better sense of how you got to this point in your life? Is it important to continue thinking about and reflecting on your past?

10

Destination:
KEEPING PERSPECTIVE

"Reality is a question of perspective."
— SALMAN RUSHDIE

CHRIS

At first I thought I'd get another job right away. But after a few weeks I got the message: getting back in the saddle isn't always just a matter of skill or willpower. The fact is, although things seemed bright at first, I didn't get any of the interest or job offers I expected, and things started looking pretty dim. This was definitely a problem, but I also knew there wasn't anything I could do about it right away. I knew that I could let this thing eat away at me or find a way to use the time I suddenly had on my hands to my advantage.

I was out of work, and that was that. So I began to read more and spent a lot more time with friends, doing things I enjoy. Although I had to go slow on my spending, I invested my time in some extra training and workshops, as well as taking care of a lot of things that I'd wanted to turn my attention to for a long time. As difficult as being unemployed was, and for lots of different reasons, I never let it get to me. Actually, I was quite sorry when I finally returned to work.

AS IMPORTANT AS work is, it is *not* the be-all and end-all of life and is certainly not the final goal for which most people strive. In fact, in spite of the value of work, the critical role it fills, and the shape it gives to life, in most cases work is a *means* to an end— not the end itself. Yet daily life has a way of wearing down our perspective and clouding our vision. As people move through their lives, they often fail to notice the track they fall into and the assumptions that mark their path. Being out of work offers many things, including the time to gain perspective and understand the fuller meaning of life beyond work.

Being out of work offers many things, including the time to gain perspective and understand the fuller meaning of life beyond work.

Assumptions

Everyone has a set of personal assumptions about himself or herself. Our self-esteem and self-image are directly influenced by those assumptions. Some people picture themselves as effective, capable, and self-directed. Others may see themselves as attractive, engaging, and successful. These beliefs are sometimes founded on actual experience, but they are also based upon a set of assumptions about yourself—the kind of person you think you are and the kind of expectations you have for yourself in life. The experiences of daily life, both satisfying and unsatisfying, can serve to alter personal assumptions, enhancing or damaging your self-esteem and self-image.

The trouble with assumptions is that they're usually unspoken and unexamined. When our assumptions about the world and the way things are, or "ought" to be, are violated, the impact can range from eye opening to disconcerting, disorienting, and earth-shattering. It all depends on how much you had invested in that set of assumptions and how much of your world and self-image was built around it.

As difficult as it may be to imagine or even consider, at this point, every adversity offers an opportunity for change. Every difficulty *forces* a situation upon you that requires a solution, and every solution offers the opportunity for personal growth. It's important to take the time to look at the assumptions you've held about yourself and how they've been affected, or shattered, by your job loss and/or your continued unemployment. Job loss provides the opportunity and the impetus to look more closely at yourself and the beliefs you've long held and decide what sort of person you are and what sort of person you want to be.

Use the next journal entry to explore how the loss of your job, and possibly continued unemployment, has affected your assumptions. What underlying, but unexplored, beliefs have you built much of your life around? What were your assumptions about work, career, and yourself?

The experiences of daily life, both satisfying and unsatisfying, can serve to alter personal assumptions, enhancing or damaging your self-esteem and self-image.

EXAMINING ASSUMPTIONS

1. What sort of assumptions did you hold about yourself before you lost this job? As you'll see, each assumption listed here is matched against another assumption that is more or less its opposite. Check off the assumptions that seem to *most* reflect the way you saw yourself or add others.

I saw myself as . . .

__an asset in any workplace	__someone with few work skills
__capable	__ineffective
__competent	__incompetent
__confident	__awkward
__emotionally solid	__emotionally fragile
__someone others would want to hire	__lucky to have a job

__successful in life   __unsuccessful in life

__successful in work/career   __unsuccessful in work/career

other: _____

_____

_____

2. Do the assumptions you've picked reflect a positive or negative self-image? Was it a

mix? _____

_____

_____

3. Pick from the following list *at least* three assumptions you held about yourself while you were working. Add others below.

__I will always have a job.   __I can depend on my employers.

__I am well thought of at work.   __I will never have to worry about unemployment.

__I can always find another job.   __There are plenty of other jobs

__I am worthwhile.   __I will be fulfilled through my work.

__I will be financially secure.   __I will be able to meet my family's needs.

__I will always have a good job.   __I will have a permanent career.

__My work will fulfill me.   __I am appreciated at work.

other: _____

_____

_____

4. What, if anything, has changed about these assumptions?

_____

_____

_____

5. Keep thinking about the assumptions you held about yourself and the sort of person you are. *Before my job loss, I assumed . . .*

_____

_____

_____

6. How have your assumptions about *yourself* changed since losing your job?

_____

_____

_____

7. What effect have damaged or changed assumptions had on your self-image?

_____

_____

_____

8. What have you learned about *yourself* through changes in your assumptions?

_____

_____

_____

9. How have you changed from this experience so far?

_____

_____

_____

THINGS TO THINK ABOUT

- What have you learned about yourself from this journal entry? Are you aware of assumptions that you *currently* hold about yourself? How can you tell if these current assumptions are correct?
- Do you think that holding assumptions sets you up for failure later? What's the alternative to assumptions?

Buying into Assumptions: "Shoulds" and "Oughts"

One of the things about assumptions is that they're often unspoken. They just *are*. Assumptions "sneak up" on people and get locked into place as the way things *should* or *ought* to be. Life gets built around these assumptions until something comes along to shatter them, sometimes leaving people feeling as though they've based their life on ideas without substance. The next entry will help you to think about *your* assumptions and where they came from. It will help you to challenge your assumptions, and, perhaps, more important, ensure that you don't simply exchange one set of assumptions for another.

BEYOND ASSUMPTIONS

1. How are things *supposed* to be?

a. *I* was *supposed to be* . . . _____

_____

b. *By now, I am supposed to be* . . . _____

_____

c. *I* should *be* . . . _____

_____

d. *Things* ought *to be* . . . _____

_____

e. *Life* should *be* . . . _____

_____

2. Who said so?

_____

_____

_____

3. Where did your assumptions come from?

_____

_____

_____

_____

4. In what ways have your assumptions helped you?

_____

_____

_____

_____

5. In what ways have your assumptions held you back?

_____

_____

_____

_____

6. What do you want to do with your assumptions?

_____

_____

_____

7. Complete these sentence starts.

a. *I was a* . . . _____

  but now, I'm a . . . _____

b. *I used to think* . . . _____

  but now, I think . . . _____

c. *I used to* . . . _____

  but now I . . . _____

Gaining Perspective

After getting knocked off your feet, it can be very difficult to gain perspective. Picking up and moving on means developing and keeping perspective so that your long-term view isn't clouded by the immediate problem.

Perspective refers to an attitude or mental outlook. For the most part, it means keeping things in proportion and seeing the *whole* picture, even though your view may be distorted by circumstances. At this time in your life, it's especially important to keep perspective, even though it may be difficult to see things clearly. There will be many things that cloud your vision, from financial worries to difficult feelings and concerns about the future. Taking back control of your future requires that you maintain perspective on the situation.

One way to keep perspective and see things clearly is to recognize that there's more to you than your job. There's also more to your life than losing your job. Just as cats have nine lives, so do people. Perhaps you're feeling as though one of those lives ended when you were fired or laid off. That still leaves you with eight more. As is often the case, there's more than one perspective here. Your other eight figurative lives can be other roles you play, interests you have in your *current* life, or other lives you'd like to live in the future.

Perspective *means keeping things in proportion and seeing the* whole *picture, even though your view may be distorted by circumstances.*

Perhaps you *are* . . .	Perhaps you'd *like* to . . .
a parent	become a writer
a musician	return to school
an athlete	get involved in a sport
a partner in a marriage	develop a whole new career
a volunteer in the community	become a consultant
an artist	lecture on job loss
an avid hobbyist	build a small business of
	your own

In the next journal entry, think about those other eight lives and what they might be. Use the entry to not only keep perspective on who you are, but to seriously consider other options for future lives and interests that can develop for you.

YOUR OTHER EIGHT LIVES

1. First give a name to the life that just ended. *My life before was as* . . . _____

_____

2. Who else are you? List eight other lives in your *current* life.

a. _____   e. _____

b. _____   f. _____

c. _____   g. _____

d. _____   h. _____

3. Of these, which ones are the most satisfying?

_____

_____

4. Which "other" lives would you like to develop further?

_____

_____

5. What prevents you from developing these other lives further?

_____

_____

6. Who else would you like to be? List eight other possible *future* lives.

a. _____   e. _____

b. _____   f. _____

c. _____   g. _____

d. _____   h. _____

7. Which of these future lives can be lived part of the time, and which ones require a full-time commitment?

_____

_____

8. Which future life would you most like to live right now?

_____

_____

9. What's stopping you from living that life now?

_____

_____

_____

THINGS TO THINK ABOUT

- Is your current life richer than you had previously imagined? Are your future interests and desires realistic? What do you need to do to make them realistic?
- Was it difficult to think of eight other present lives and eight future lives? Why? What limits your ability to consider other aspects of your current life or imagine other futures for yourself?
- Are the constraints and responsibilities of your present life interfering with your ability to live a different life in the future? If so, how can you responsibly make changes in your current life that allow future change?

Using Your Time

In keeping with the idea that there's more to you than your lost job, this free time you now have can be used in any number of ways. No matter how much effort you put into finding a new job, your actual job search won't take up all of your time. What will the rest of your life be like each day, and what will it be like for your spouse and kids or your friends and other important relationships? What will happen to your other interests and your mental and physical health? The fact is that you have a life outside of work and now have had the gift of time to do other things.

Use the next entry to think about these other things you've wanted to do, but haven't had the time (or perspective) to do—until now! This entry will help you better understand both those things and yourself. After you've written your list, use the keys below to organize, code, and better understand the list.

FIFTY THINGS

1. Create a list of fifty things to do after job loss. Create your whole list *first*, writing one item on each line provided until you've named all fifty of the things you want to do.

2. Once you've written the entire list, return to each item and assign it to one of these categories:

ED: Educational (returning to school, taking courses or workshops, etc.)

FA: Family (family-centered activity involving spouse, kids, or other important family members)

FP: Fun/Play (travel, sports, or leisure, for instance)

IS: Identity/Self-Esteem (resolving old issues, getting fit, or accepting new challenges)

JR: Job Related (seeking work, job retraining, and network building)

MH: Mental Health (counseling, therapy, or attending a support group)

MT: Maintenance Tasks (painting the house, spring cleaning, etc.)

MO: Financial (budgeting, investing, or financial security)

PH: Physical Health (things that are intended to improve or maintain your health)
PI: Personal Improvement (reading, learning a new skill, etc.)
RE: Relationships (things directly connected to building or maintaining relationships)
SR: Spiritual/Reflective (things that are most associated with a search for meaning)
OT: Other (things that can't be placed under any other category)

3. Next, prioritize each item as:

A: crucial
B: important
C: less important
D: dispensable

4. Finally, assign a time line for when you'd like to do each thing:

1: within twenty-four hours
2: within a week
3: within a month
4: within a year
5: no time limit

Thing I Want to Do	Category	Priority	Time Line
1.			
2.			
3.			
4.			
5.			
6.			
7.			
8.			
9.			
10.			
11.			
12.			

Thing I Want to Do	Category	Priority	Time Line
13.			
14.			
15.			
16.			
17.			
18.			
19.			
20.			
21.			
22.			
23.			
24.			
25.			
26.			
27.			
28.			
29.			
30.			
31.			
32.			
33.			
34.			
35.			
36.			
37.			

Thing I Want to Do	Category	Priority	Time Line
38. _____	_____	_____	_____
39. _____	_____	_____	_____
40. _____	_____	_____	_____
41. _____	_____	_____	_____
42. _____	_____	_____	_____
43. _____	_____	_____	_____
44. _____	_____	_____	_____
45. _____	_____	_____	_____
46. _____	_____	_____	_____
47. _____	_____	_____	_____
48. _____	_____	_____	_____
49. _____	_____	_____	_____
50. _____	_____	_____	_____

5. Take a look at your pattern of choices. How many of your choices were related to spending time with your family, how many were play items, and so on? Tally up the way you classified each thing here.

__Educational   __Family   __Fun/Play

__Identity/Self-Esteem __ Job Related   __Mental Health

__Maintenance Tasks   __Financial   __Physical Health

__Personal Improvement __Relationships   __Spiritual/Reflective

__Other

6. Do you notice a pattern? Is there an even distribution of things in every category, or do most items fall into two or three areas? Describe the pattern.

_____

_____

_____

7. What does your list tell you about yourself?

_____

_____

_____

_____

_____

_____

_____

_____

_____

8. Now look at your "priority" and "time line" scores. What patterns do you see here, and what does it tell you about yourself?

_____

_____

_____

_____

_____

_____

_____

_____

_____

THINGS TO THINK ABOUT

- How high a priority are relationships, especially _family_ relationships?
- Are there high priority items on your list that you never seem to get to? If so, why do these high priority items seem to keep getting bumped?
- Are you ready to start doing some of the things on your list? If not, why not?

Checkpoint: Keeping Perspective

Keeping perspective on who you are and what's important requires the commitment and ability to tune in to your surroundings and yourself.

As you near completion of this chapter, the work in which you're now engaged actively involves self-assessment and strengthening the ground upon which you're making both current and future decisions. As you begin to better understand yourself, your needs and the needs of your family (if relevant), and choices available to you, it will be important to keep your values clearly in mind.

Keeping perspective on who you are and what's important requires the commitment and ability to tune in to your surroundings and yourself. The final entry in the chapter runs over fifteen consecutive days and will help you to focus on what's important and what isn't. This journal entry is more akin to the "classic" journal, as it involves free-form writing, but for each day the exercise is based on a single question.

For the next fifteen evenings freewrite for ten to fifteen minutes using only the question posed as your guide for that day. Each question is repeated three times during the course of the exercise. Write your entry each evening in a separate journal or on a separate sheet of paper, and use the entry below to summarize and reflect upon your thoughts and experiences over the entire exercise. Complete Steps 2 through 5 *after* the end of the fifteen days.

In many ways a writing exercise like this requires more of you, not only because it asks for at least ten minutes of writing, but because it requires you to focus in on yourself and your day, taking the time to think about what's happening in your life and what's important.

KEEPING PERSPECTIVE

1. For the next fifteen days, freewrite for ten to fifteen minutes using the following questions as the basis for your entry each day. Write each entry in a separate journal or on a separate sheet of paper.

- Nights 1, 6, and 11:   *What's important to me is . . .*
- Nights 2, 7, and 12:   *What I want to do at this point in my life is . . .*
- Nights 3, 8, and 13:   *What I do well is . . .*
- Nights 4, 9, and 14:   *What I love to do is . . .*
- Nights 5, 10, and 15:   *What I've learned about myself is . . .*

2. At the end of the fifteen days, reread what you've written for each day. Briefly summarize your thoughts and experiences for each day below. Notice that this question doesn't run in *chronological* order, but groups your entry by the type of question asked each day.

Night 1: *What's important to me is . . .* _____

_____

Night 6: *What's important to me is . . .* _____

_____

Night 11: *What's important to me is . . .* _____

_____

Night 2: *What I want to do at this point in my life is . . .* _____

_____

Night 7: *What I want to do at this point in my life is . . .* _____

_____

Night 12: *What I want to do at this point in my life is . . .* _____

_____

Night 3: *What I do well is . . .* _____

_____

Night 8: *What I do well is . . .* _____

_____

Night 13: *What I do well is . . .* _____

_____

Night 4: *What I love to do is . . .* _____

_____

Night 9: *What I love to do is . . .* _____

_____

Night 14: *What I love to do is . . .* _____

_____

Night 5: *What I've learned about myself is . . .* _____

_____

Night 10: *What I've learned about myself is . . .* _____

_____

Night 15: *What I've learned about myself is . . .* _____

_____

3. Summarize your entire experience over the past fifteen days.

_____

_____

_____

_____

_____

_____

4. What have you learned about yourself?

_____

_____

_____

_____

_____

_____

5. What seems most important at this time in your life?

_____

_____

_____

_____

_____

_____

_____

_____

_____

_____

_____

_____

_____

THINGS TO THINK ABOUT

- Was it difficult to freewrite in this way, or was it a rewarding and effective way to check in with yourself each day?
- If you continue to freewrite in this way, is it useful to pose a question to be answered each day?
- Do you feel as though you have the "right" perspective on all this? Do you have a perspective that is helpful to you at this time, rather than hindering you?

I I

Destination:
MONEY

CAROL

Money was always important in my life. I never really even knew it, because it was always there. I grew up in an affluent family and never had to think about money, or financial survival. After graduate school, I became a successful accountant and built a pretty successful business for myself. Money wasn't the reason I had success, but I just never realized how it always sort of played a role in the background of my life. My decisions in life, I realized later, were often built around earning money, and personal satisfaction was somehow connected to always having money and always earning more.

After my business failed, I was amazed that I couldn't just step into another job. I wasn't the "right" one for this job, or didn't have the "right" attitude for that one. In some cases, I'm sure I didn't get a second glance because of approaching middle age. After a while, I actually started worrying about money. It wasn't that I didn't have enough, even if I wasn't working. But, it was the plain fact that my income had provided both emotional comfort and become the yard-stick by which I measured my success, my well-being, and my value. Without it, I began to feel depressed and quite dejected.

I'm working again of course, but haven't forgotten the lessons learned. I direct a lot more of my energy now at doing both the things money can buy, and the things it can't begin to touch.

THERE'S AN OLD Jack Benny routine that exemplified a common relationship people have with money. In it, he's approached by a mugger who demands, "Your money or your life." Benny responds with silence, and the mugger repeats, "Your money or your life." Again, the mugger is greeted with silence. Agitated now, the mugger says, "I said, 'Your money or your life.'" This time Jack Benny answers him. "Wait a minute. I'm thinking."

There's no way to overestimate the power of money to make us feel better and to make us think that if only we had more of it our lives would be immeasurably improved. At the same time, we should never *under*estimate money. One of the first things you had to deal with upon losing your job was the loss of your income and the anxiety that accompanied that final paycheck. For many people, money is the *first* priority. The race to find another job is often more a race against declining savings and the possibility of backed-up bills than a search for the ideal job.

Despite the obvious reasons why money is such a basic need and so critical to most people, it's still important to understand in what other ways it's so critical. The primary focus of this chapter is to help you think about and understand your relationship with money.

An Old Story about Money

One day, a poor beggar who had just been given a loaf of bread noticed an old woman with an infant asking for handouts. "Here," he said, handing her the bread, "you need this more than I do." Later that evening, he heard a knocking at the door of his shack in the woods. When he opened the door, there stood an angel in white robes. "Because of your generosity," the angel said, "you have been sent this magical purse. Whenever you put your hand in it, you will find a gold coin. No matter how many coins you remove, it will always contain another. That is, until you spend one. Once you have spent one of the golden coins, the purse will stop producing." The angel handed the poor man the purse, then vanished. Slowly, the beggar stuck his hand into the purse. There was a gold coin. He stuck his hand in again. There was another coin. He took it out and put his hand in again. Out came another coin, then another, and another, and another. "Ah," he said, "perhaps I should go buy a hot roll." But then he thought, "If I go and buy a hot roll, the purse will stop making gold coins." So he spent the night without eating and in the morning went out to beg for a few coins. He thought, "I will keep taking gold coins out of the purse for a few more days, then I'll take one and go out and have a good meal." But each time he was about to go out and spend one of the coins, the thought of the purse no longer working upset him, and he would get by on his meager income from begging. Years later, when he died of old age, exposure, and malnutrition, the police found thousands of gold coins hidden in every nook and cranny of his little cabin. They used one to pay for a simple coffin and tombstone, and the rest were taken into the town treasury.

We often give money more power than it has, claiming that financial concerns control our behavior. In this story, the old man continued to live his life as though he had no money. His fears of once again being poor, and his goal of having "enough" money, kept him poor. How much does *not* having money hold you back? How much does *having* money hold you back?

Use the next journal entry to reflect on the story of the old man and the coins and your own fears about not having enough money.

AN OLD STORY ABOUT MONEY

1. How much does money control your life?

_____

_____

_____

2. Does money control your life more than you'd like it to? If so, how?

_____

_____

_____

3. Does a fear of not having money prevent you from living your life more fully?

_____

_____

_____

4. If you had a magic purse like the old man in the story, when would you have *enough* money so you could relax and enjoy your life?

_____

_____

_____

5. What role does money play in your life?

_____

_____

_____

6. Can you live a rewarding and satisfying life, even on a reduced income?

_____

_____

_____

7. When you have money, do fears of not having enough or being without money hold you back from living more freely?

_____

_____

_____

The Meaning of Money

Money means vastly different things to different people. For some, money is just a means to an end—the entire reason for earning money is so you can buy the things you need or want. For others, money *is* the end, representing security and filling an emotional need. In some cases, money is a means to earn still more money, and in other cases, money is a means for gaining control in a chaotic world. Money, for some, is more a measure of power.

Money has become the source of inspiration, incentive, and equity upon and through which things get produced. Money has been a source of political control and argument since it was invented, giving rise to ideologies and entire political systems. Money is *probably* the reason you lost your job, and money has undoubtedly become one of your major concerns since you lost your job. Money, then, is something that people have an important relationship with, no matter what that relationship is. For the writer, James Baldwin, "Money, it turned out, was exactly like sex, you thought of nothing else if you didn't have it and thought of other things if you did."

Do you ever think about *your* relationship with money? Is it a blessing or the root of all evil? Is money something that merely enhances your life, or is it something you can't live without?

THE MEANING OF MONEY

1. *Money is . . .* _____

2. *Having money means . . .* _____

3. *Being without money means . . .* _____

4. *To me, money represents . . .*

___ affirmation: a concrete statement about my worth and value

___ autonomy: the freedom to do what I want without answering to others

___ control: the ability to control my own destiny

___ confidence: the feeling that I'm as good as anyone else

___ dignity: being able to go anywhere, head held high

___ freedom: the ability to do what I want without being beholden to anyone else

___ independence: the ability to decide what I want to do, and when

___ love: being able to care for and give affection to others

___ nurturance: being cared for and given affection

___ power: the ability to control other people's behavior

___ respect: the admiration of others

___ security: the feeling of being safe and protected

___ success: a concrete statement about my ability to be as good or better than others

other: _____

_____

_____

5. Being without money means . . .

___denial: the need to deny myself or my family the things we want or need

___dependence: the inability to stand fully on my own feet

___discomfort: constant sense of being under pressure

___envy: the feeling that others have what I wish I could have, or should have

___failure: a statement of my inability to be successful or as good as others

___insecurity: fears that I won't be able to manage if things go wrong

___misery: the feeling that nothing is right

___powerlessness: a sense that there's nothing I can do if things go the wrong way

___servitude: the requirement to always work for others and do what they want

___shame: the feeling of not being good enough

___worthlessness: the feeling of not being good enough

other: _____

_____

_____

6. What's *your* relationship with money?

_____

_____

_____

_____

7. Can you live without it? Why or why not?

_____

_____

_____

_____

_____

Financial Reality

Having said all this about relationships and the symbolic meaning of money, it's certainly pie in the sky to think that money isn't important in your life. In fact, although this chapter is late in the book, you may be coming to it early. One of the first and most immediate concerns people have when they are laid off is financial survival following job loss. Often, the first image in people's mind when they get a pink slip, or when they hear that their spouse has just gotten a pink slip, is of being driven away from their home with their children, clutching a few special possessions.

In light of your specific situation as an unemployed person, the *major* reason for considering your relationship with money right now is so that you can continue to live a meaningful, satisfying, and productive life even without the level of income you formerly had. Beyond putting money in its place, it's important for you to be considering how to manage financial resources that have now become quite scarce. This usually means a financial plan of some kind.

By this point in your recovery and rebuilding work, you certainly should have developed and be using some sort of financial plan to help get you get through your immediate situation, while developing more substantial plans for the future. If you haven't, then you're either floating along with reduced resources, or you're really struggling with money, in which case you need to get some outside help at once. There are *many* resources that can help you to analyze and develop financial plans and budgets.

If you are struggling with financial pressures and realities, all the thinking, discussion, and self-exploration in the world will do little to alleviate the situation, unless you're seriously prepared to significantly alter your lifestyle (and the lifestyle of your family, if you're married). Otherwise, you may need some concrete outside help. There are many professionally written self-help books and tapes available, as well as accountants and financial counselors, that can help you analyze your situation and plan carefully. One thing to avoid is leaning on credit too heavily, or leaning on the wrong kind of credit. Running up credit card bills, for instance, may help today, but can exhaust your savings or wipe you out later.

If you are having financial difficulties, think about getting help at once.

Despite the difficulty of managing life with a reduced income, consider carefully all the motivational forces in your life at this time, beyond money.

Putting Money in Its Place

How much does money, your concern about it, and your drive to not be without it affect your life at this time? Is it shaping your life, and is it the most important thing? Or, are there other, more important driving forces in your life? What motivates you when you think of earning and saving money? Are you clear about how to live your life with or without money?

We're always put in the position of making choices. Despite the difficulty of managing life with a reduced income, consider carefully *all* the motivational forces in your life at this time, beyond money. Take the time to think carefully about the decisions you make, the things that you want or allow to shape those decisions, and the way you want to live your life. Use the last journal entry in this chapter to think about how to best tuck money into a healthy place in your life.

A HEALTHY APPRECIATION

1. What constitutes a healthy appreciation for money?

___ an understanding of your attitude toward money

___ earning and having money, without condemning or worshiping it

___ refusing to sacrifice moral or ethical standards for money

___ the ability to use money to improve your life and the lives of those around you

___ the ability to use money without being used by it

___ using money to provide for pleasure as well as necessities

other: _____

_____

2. Conversely, what would constitute an unhealthy attitude or relationship with money?

_____

_____

_____

_____

3. How has your attitude toward or relationship with money shaped and affected your life until now?

_____

_____

_____

_____

4. Has that relationship changed much since losing your job? How?

_____

_____

_____

_____

5. How has your attitude and appreciation for money affected the life of your spouse and children, if you're married?

_____

_____

_____

_____

6. What's the most important thing for you about money?

_____

_____

_____

_____

7. What's the least important thing?

_____

_____

_____

_____

8. What's the most important thing you've learned about money since losing your job?

_____

_____

_____

_____

9. What has money taught you about yourself?

_____

_____

_____

_____

THINGS TO THINK ABOUT

- Do you need to make changes in your relationship with or attitude about money? Are you in control of the money in your life, or is it in control of you?
- Do you believe that money should be an important and useful supplement to your life, or the driving force? Do you have some other beliefs about money and the role it should play in your life?
- Has money helped you achieve your most meaningful goals, or can these be accomplished without having any money at all? Has money stood in the way of accomplishing meaningful personal goals?

12

Destination:
NETWORKING

"There are three kinds of death in this world. There's heart death, there's brain death, and there's being off the network."
—GUY ALMES

TED

After looking through the newspapers for weeks, going to the local unemployment service, and signing up with a couple of job-search agencies, I finally realized that finding a job that way was depending way too much on being in the right place at the right time, waiting for someone to contact me. I'd certainly heard about networking, and I decided this was a plunge I had to take. Although I didn't know exactly how to go about it, I knew that using a network meant taking the bull by the horns and putting myself in the right place. I was going to contact them.

I started calling everyone I knew, and pretty soon learned to overcome my own timidity and embarrassment. After a couple of weeks, I was calling everyone, including my old boss (the guy who fired me). Each time I called someone I made sure to get the names of a few other people I might call. It was definitely tough at first, and most leads went nowhere, but I learned a lot about what was out there. After a while, building and working my network became a job for me.

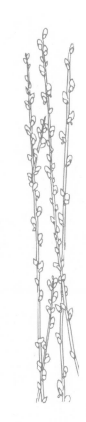

BACK IN CHAPTER 6 ("Destination: Support"), a network was described as a system of interconnected people. However, in that chapter, the network was used to describe your system of support. The word is more commonly used to describe a professional or collegial chain of people or organizations, connected and interacting in some way to serve some specified need or goal.

In the case of the Internet, the World Wide Web *is* the network, linking and forming associations between people and organizations literally all over the world. That network is used to exchange information, sell products, and connect people with like interests. That network has made people wealthy, and it has educated and connected people in ways not formerly possible.

In the case of career development and job search, the "network" now represents an informal chain of people, connected to one another through a shared *professional* link and, more important, a chain of *people*. The job-search network is informal because it doesn't involve fees, professional employment agencies, headhunters, or a response to an advertised or otherwise posted position. In fact, the network, in this case, rests primarily upon who you know, or who you can *get* to know.

Once upon a time, this sort of connection was referred to as "the old boys club," known as an exclusionary and elitist chain that kept outsiders outside. This is partially still true. That is, you have to be, or know, an insider to get into the network. But today, more than ever, you can build your own network. Networking has become a powerful, and increasingly common, way to find jobs that are often unadvertised and might otherwise be invisible to you. There are many resources available to you for learning how to develop and use a network, or how to tie into and take advantage of existing networks. This chapter will help you to explore the ideas and methods of network development and decide if networking is for you.

In the case of career development and job search, the "network" now represents an informal chain of people, connected to one another through a shared professional *link, and more important, a chain of* people.

Posting Yourself on the Network

For many reasons, it isn't always easy for people to "sell" themselves. Sometimes, they're just not assertive enough. Other times, they don't know *how* to sell themselves, don't *want* to sell themselves, or just feel awkward.

The first step in any job search is organizing your resume. In its broadest sense, a resume is a description of your strengths, skills, and experiences. It's often the basis for getting an interview, which, of course, is usually the basis for getting a job. Similarly, the first step in network building is preparing a list of those things you have to offer someone out there. Use this first entry to think about your skills and interests and, perhaps more to the point, how you feel about "selling" these to people out there in the network.

MARKETING YOURSELF

1. List at least five of your skills in each area:

Personal Skills	Work Skills	Other Skills
_____	_____	_____
_____	_____	_____
_____	_____	_____
_____	_____	_____
_____	_____	_____
_____	_____	_____

2. List at least five of your primary strengths:

_____	_____	_____
_____	_____	_____

3. Write a brief description of what you do well.

_____

_____

_____

_____

_____

4. Why would someone want to hire you?

_____

_____

_____

_____

5. How do you feel about marketing yourself to people?

_____

_____

_____

_____

6. What's the hardest part about marketing yourself?

_____

_____

_____

_____

7. What's the easiest part?

_____

_____

_____

_____

8. What's the most important part?

_____

_____

_____

9. What does it feel like to have to sell yourself?

_____

_____

_____

THINGS TO THINK ABOUT

- Do you feel that you're a worthwhile candidate for a job? Were you able to come up with important skills that you can market? If not, why not, and how can you either improve your actual skills or improve your ability to describe them to others?
- Does *actively* looking for a job, as in networking, make you feel like you're "selling" yourself? Is it okay with you to have to do this?

Your Community Is Your Network

After developing a clear sense of what you have to offer and how you *feel* about marketing yourself to others, you have to find people to market yourself to. One way to do this, of course, is through responding to job advertisements in newspapers, at an office, or on the Internet. An additional route taken by more and more people, and a direct route sometimes to jobs not even otherwise posted, is through a network of people.

Some people already have a network. Others buy names and addresses through network services. Most have to build their network from scratch. This may seem daunting and, if you don't already have a network in place, this will require time, effort, energy, and patience to develop a really effective network. Chances are you already *have* a network or the beginnings of one.

After developing a clear sense of what you have to offer and how you feel *about marketing yourself to others, you have to find people to market yourself to.*

A network is no more than a community of people who interact. Ideally, that community would contain *only* those people who can actually offer you a job. But in most cases the network is full of people who are able to help you spread yourself out further and further, directing and linking you to people who *are* able to offer you work.

A network is no more than a community of people who interact.

We all live in multiple communities. For most, there are at least geographical, social, and work/professional communities. If you're an architect living in New York City, who loves to bowl on Friday nights, go to sports events on the weekend, works out at a local health club, and writes songs on the side, you belong to many communities. You not only live in the community of New York, but you also belong to a professional community of architects and various other communities of friends, colleagues, and associates who share your interests. Each of these is a possible community of links that can serve as initial or important connections to a larger, expanding network.

YOUR COMMUNITY NETWORK

1. Think of all the types of people through whom you can make connections.

__ acquaintances   __ colleagues   __ colleagues of colleagues

__ family   __ family friends   __ fellow club members

__ former bosses   __ friends   __ friends' friends

__ neighbors   __ neighbors' friends   __ spouse's friends

__ sports teammates   others: _____

2. List any organizations you belong to or participate in.

_____   _____

_____   _____

_____   _____

3. List other organizations you would consider joining.

_____   _____

_____   _____

_____   _____

4. List annual meetings, training sessions, study groups, or other places you might meet people who could help you.

_____   _____

_____   _____

_____   _____

5. Are there support groups you can join for displaced workers or "outplacement" services available through your former employer or local unemployment office?

_____   _____

_____   _____

6. What will it be like to contact and talk to people you don't necessarily know well?

_____

_____

_____

7. What will it be like to let these people know that you're looking for work?

_____

_____

_____

8. How will you deal with any feelings that may arise for you?

_____

_____

_____

_____

- Does the idea of building a network excite or tire you? Will building and using a network help you to find a job?
- Can you find work without using a network? Will a network help the process?
- Is the idea of soliciting work and/or contacts through friends comfortable, or uncomfortable for you? How can you best deal with any discomfort?

Using Your Network

The goal of networking is to help you get a new job. Nevertheless, beyond finding a job right now, networking is a lifelong experience that continues far beyond a single job. Even when you are employed, networking keeps you in touch with your field and on top of opportunities that may be out there, helping to ensure against future job loss.

Many people are reluctant to use a network, but having a network is of little use unless you activate it. Usually, people have to "work" their network to get results. Contacting one person on the network can give you a lead to three other people, and each of those three can lead to many more leads. In this way, as your network expands exponentially, so does your knowledge of what's out there, along with your chances of finding a new job.

Contacting one person on the network can give you a lead to three other people, and each of those three can lead to many more leads.

The next journal entry spans five weeks and is designed to help you initiate and experiment with networking. For the entry, you'll network with nine people each week, for a total of (at least) forty-five contacts over the five-week period. That may sound like a lot, but that's less than two people each business day of the week. That's probably far less work than you were doing each day when you were employed, and now you really *are* working for yourself.

If you find the experience useful and fulfilling, continue networking after the exercise has ended. No matter what, you'll better understand networking, yourself, and how this sort of process fits your style and needs. For this entry, list nine people you will contact each week. Add to the list each week as you make more contacts through your existing network and your network expands. At the end of each networking week, use the entry to briefly describe your experience.

FORTY-FIVE CONTACTS

Network Week 1

1. List your nine contacts for this week.

_____   _____   _____

_____   _____   _____

_____   _____   _____

2. a. What was the most useful part of the experience?

_____

_____

b. What was the most difficult part?

_____

_____

3. What did you learn about networking?

_____

_____

_____

4. Were you able to develop contacts for your next network week?

_____

5. Was this is a satisfying week?

_____

Network Week 2

1. List your nine contacts for this week.

_____   _____   _____

_____   _____   _____

_____   _____   _____

2. a. What was the most useful part of the experience?

_____

_____

b. What was the most difficult part?

_____

_____

3. What did you learn about networking?

_____

_____

_____

4. Were you able to develop contacts for your next network week?

_____

5. Was this week easier or more difficult than last week?

_____

6. Are you motivated to continue, or are you discouraged?

_____

Network Week 3

1. List your nine contacts for this week.

_____   _____   _____

_____   _____   _____

_____   _____   _____

2. Describe the networking experience so far.

_____

_____

3. What are you learning about yourself?

_____

_____

_____

4. Have you been able to steadily develop new network contacts each week?

_____

5. Is it getting easier to network?

_____

6. Does networking seem useful?

_____

Network Week 4

1. List your nine contacts for this week.

_____   _____   _____

_____   _____   _____

_____   _____   _____

2. What are you learning about your network?

_____

_____

_____

3. What are you learning about the job market?

_____

_____

_____

4. Is your network expanding?

_____

5. Is it getting easier or more difficult to network?

_____

Network Week 5

1. List your nine contacts for this week.

_____   _____   _____

_____   _____   _____

_____   _____   _____

2. What have you learned about yourself over the last five weeks?

_____

_____

_____

_____

3. Has networking added to your life in any way? If so, how? If not, why not?

_____

_____

_____

_____

THINGS TO THINK ABOUT

- Is networking your style? Have you found it to be an important experience? Is networking something that you'll continue to do? Why or why not?
- What has networking taught you about yourself? What have you learned about finding a job? What have you learned about networks?

Staying in Touch

Even if networking isn't for you, for whatever reason, it's still important to use your network to stay in touch with people in your life. Unemployment can be especially stifling and dispiriting if it removes and isolates you from friends, acquaintances, and colleagues outside of your immediate circle. Use this time—and your network—to stay in touch.

Here your task is not to use people in your extended network to find a job. It's simply to stay connected and to maintain the important connections in your life. Call someone you know and say hello. Have lunch with someone you haven't had lunch with for a long time. Have a dinner party. Attend a conference or seminar where you'll run into old friends.

Use the final entry in this chapter to reflect upon the importance or value of the network in your life.

It's important to use your network to stay in touch with people in your life.

CONNECTIONS

1. Are you satisfied with your network? In what ways are you satisfied?

_____

_____

_____

_____

2. In what ways is your network most important to you?

_____

_____

_____

3. How might you expand your network so that it better meets your needs?

_____

_____

_____

13

Destination:
SEEING YOUR LIFE WITH
FRESH EYES

"Our life is what our thoughts make it."
—MARCUS AURELIUS

MARION

After I lost my college teaching position, I couldn't stop thinking about what I could have done differently, and how I should have planned better. It's not easy to find a job in this field, and I felt sort of desperate about finding a new position. It seemed as though losing my job had ruined my life. I attended seminar after seminar, not only to stay in touch with the field but also to make new contacts and find work leads. But something that a keynote speaker at one particular conference said really made sense to me, and took hold in a way I never imagined it would.

The speaker discussed emotional health and relationships as the most important tools and the basis for a satisfying life. She never discussed work or money or status. Instead, she talked about the ability to "let go," and what she said made so much sense. After that conference I began to do just that. I felt as though I was thinking more clearly and more realistically, putting things into a new perspective. I not only was able to better appreciate and take pleasure from those parts of my life that hadn't changed, but my vision became clearer and my goals more focused. I was able to let go and look at things in a way that was rational and helpful, not irrational and hurtful.

MUCH OF YOUR journaling work so far has dealt with the practical and emotional consequences of job loss: adjustment, management, and gaining perspective and insight. But as you begin to move away from reactions to job loss to more careful planning and decisions about your future, it will be important to step outside of the requirements, tasks, and routines of your daily life to ensure that you have the capacity to reflect upon and contemplate your life and what you want for yourself and your family.

In this chapter, the goal is to help you slow down your world, look at it from a different angle, and inject new ideas and ways of approaching problems into your daily life. The work in this chapter will help you see your life in a new way not only as you continue to rebuild after job loss, but in every area of your life and in every way.

Learning to see those things that might normally be invisible to you, hidden under the burdens of everyday living or blended seamlessly into the background texture of your life, is quite literally an "eye-opening" experience.

The Importance of Fresh Thinking

Fresh thinking, or the ability to look at things in a new light, is important to you at *every* point along all of your journeys. But the ability to step outside your situation and see things from a different perspective is especially pertinent right now as you tackle the Stage 3 tasks of assessment and planning and begin to deal with, the Stage 4 issues of decision making and self-renewal.

It is important to begin than with an exploration of those things that lie in the background of your own life. Learning to see those things that might normally be invisible to you, hidden under the burdens of everyday living or blended seamlessly into the background texture of your life, is quite literally an "eye-opening" experience. Such new vision can help you see more deeply, think more clearly, and make better and more well-rounded decisions in all areas of your life as you continue to define your own future.

Slowing Down and Contemplation

Part of finding a new approach often involves slowing down, not only to find time to "smell the roses," but also so life doesn't just whiz past at it's normally high rate. When we're used to things moving at one speed and being one way we often see just the "big" picture, missing the small details that lie underneath or off to one side.

Slowing down means getting off the bus of daily life for a moment. In this quieter and slower place, you have the time to consider the world you live in and *how* you live in it, discover for yourself what has value and what works best for you, and think about things that don't always have answers. The ability to explore feelings without becoming passionate, to consider the world without taking action, and to speak to yourself without words is perhaps the essence of contemplation. This act of looking inside helps you to know yourself, to understand how you effect and are affected by the world outside.

The ability to explore feelings without becoming passionate, to consider the world without taking action, and to speak to yourself without words is perhaps the essence of contemplation.

Gathering Inspiration

Each chapter in this book opens with a quotation of some sort, and other quotes are spread throughout the text. There's a good reason for this. Quotations often manage to set exactly the right tone and help frame an idea and are frequently sources for inspiration and personal motivation. Quotations can exactly capture your feelings, sharply focus your thoughts, or put into words a thought you could not previously express.

Quotations can provoke, challenge, stimulate, penetrate, shame, and make us laugh. They are often tiny pearls of wisdom. Look over the quotations in this book, think about other favorite quotations, or look for quotations, passages in books, poetry verses, or lines from songs that move, inspire, motivate, capture your thoughts or feelings, or in some other way affect you. For the next journal entry think about words that have significance and meaning for you.

WORDS OF WISDOM

1. Select three favorite or otherwise meaningful quotations and copy each here.

a. _____

_____

_____

b. _____

_____

_____

c. _____

_____

_____

2. Pick one of these quotations for this entry. _____

3. Why did you select this particular quotation for this entry?

_____

_____

_____

4. How do these words have relevance to your life at this time?

_____

_____

_____

_____

5. What do these words mean to you?

_____

_____

_____

_____

6. In what ways can these words instruct you or offer you direction?

_____

_____

_____

_____

THINGS TO THINK ABOUT

- Were you able to find three quotations that moved you? Was it difficult to find three or difficult to limit yourself to *only* three?
- Were you able to you understand *why* the quotation you chose for the entry affected you? Can this quote help you find direction or strength at this time in your life?
- Was this a useful journal entry? Can you continue to find inspiration in the words of others? Will you continue to search out and record the words and thoughts of others?

Picturing Your Life

People often don't notice the things that lie in the background of their lives, even though these things may contribute to their well-being every day in some way. These can be people, places, or things, and might include important relationships, a favorite time of the day or the view from a window, a lovely home or a peaceful garden, or physical health and well-being. These things simply slip out of our consciousness because they're there all the time. Sometimes we're simply not looking for them, and other times we just take them for granted.

People often don't notice the things that lie in the background of their lives, even though these things may contribute to their well-being every day in some way.

These things are very important and are often noticed only *after* they're gone. Sometimes a dramatic situation, such as a life-threatening illness in a family member, brings something important, but normally unnoticed, to the surface. But after the crisis has passed, the importance of this relationship once again settles into the background where it's again almost lost. Other times we miss something only after it's permanently lost.

In these next three journal entries, you'll have the chance to look for and pay attention to some of those things that are usually in the background of your life. For this series of entries you'll need a camera, but a cheap, disposable camera is absolutely fine. This entry, and the two that follow, runs over a six-day period, and the entries themselves are used to summarize the entire six days.

THE CAMERA'S EYE

In this entry, you'll take one photograph each day of something that has value for you at this time in your life. The photo can be of a thing, a place, or a person. It can be a still life, an action shot, a portrait, a self-portrait, or any shot that manages to capture an image you value. For this entry, take only *one* photograph each day.

It may difficult to take a photo of some of the things you value. For instance, if you value the emotional support offered to you by a family member or a friend, you'll have to think about how to best capture that *feeling* on film. If it's a favorite piece of music or affirming thought from a book, it may be challenging to figure out how to somehow record the experience on film. For each day of the entry, find something of special value in your life right *now*.

1. Think of things, places, and people that you value in your life. List five of each.

Important Things	Important Places	Important People
a. _____	_____	_____
b. _____	_____	_____
c. _____	_____	_____

Important Things	Important Places	Important People
d. _____	_____	_____
e. _____	_____	_____

Was it easy to find five things of each type, or was it difficult? If it was difficult, or you were unable to list five of each type, why? _____

_____

_____

_____

2. For each of the six days, find something that you really value. It can be anything. If you like, use the list you just created as a "tickler." You can look at the list each day and use it to find inspiration for that day, or just be open that day to whatever presents itself as important. But remember, you can take only *one* photo each day, so think before you shoot. If you find something else important *after* you've taken your photograph, think about taking a photo of it the next day.

3. At the end of each day, complete the part of this entry that deals with that day only. After you've completed the entire six-day exercise, develop your film and complete the final part of the entry.

DAY I

Day: _____ Date: _____

a. What did you photograph today?_____

b. Why was this your choice?_____

c. What's important about this thing?_____

d. Has it *always* been important?_____

e. Why is it important *now*?_____

f. What does this important object say about you?_____

_____

DAY 2

Day: _____ Date:_____

a. What did you photograph today?_____

b. Why was this your choice?_____

c. What's important about this thing?_____

d. Has it *always* been important?_____

e. Why is it important *now*?_____

f. What does this important object say about you?_____

_____

DAY 3

Day: _____ Date:_____

a. What did you photograph today?_____

b. Why was this your choice?_____

c. What's important about this thing?_____

d. Has it *always* been important?_____

e. Why is it important *now*?_____

f. What does this important object say about you?_____

_____

DAY 4

Day: _____ Date:_____

a. What did you photograph today?_____

b. Why was this your choice?_____

c. What's important about this thing?_____

d. Has it *always* been important?_____

e. Why is it important *now*?_____

f. What does this important object say about you?_____

_____

DAY 5

Day: _____ Date: _____

a. What did you photograph today?_____

b. Why was this your choice?_____

c. What's important about this thing?_____

d. Has it *always* been important?_____

e. Why is it important *now*?_____

f. What does this important object say about you?_____

_____

DAY 6

Day: _____ Date: _____

a. What did you photograph today?_____

b. Why was this your choice?_____

c. What's important about this thing?_____

d. Has it *always* been important?_____

e. Why is it important *now*?_____

f. What does this important object say about you?_____

_____

4. After completing the six days, get your film developed. Line each photo into the order in which it was shot. Do you see any relationship between the things you pho-

tographed? Are they all similar things, or quite different? For instance, perhaps all the photos are of people. Perhaps you chose all things or places for your shots.

_____

_____

_____

_____

5. Of the six photos taken, pick three that represent those things in your life that are most important. Which three did you pick, and why?

Photo   Reason for Importance

a. _____   _____

                                         _____

b. _____   _____

                                         _____

c. _____   _____

                                         _____

6. What has this journal entry helped you to focus on in your life?

_____

_____

_____

_____

The Changing Picture of Your Life

Your life isn't static. It changes over time, sometimes in ways you want it to and sometimes in ways you'd rather it didn't change. In many cases, you may not even realize that it has changed. In the previous entry, you focused your attention and thoughts on those things that are currently important in your life. Now, in this next entry, set your sights on something that *used* to be important, but now has no has value for you. Again, your photo can be of a thing, a place, or a person.

Like the previous journal entry, this entry runs over six days. Once again, complete the relevant portion of the entry each night, and finish the entry only at the end of the six-day period. To keep this journal entry separate from your last entry, finish the previous entry *before* coming to this entry. Don't use the same roll of film. As in the last entry, take only *one* photograph each day.

THROUGH THE CAMERA'S EYE AGAIN

For this entry, take a photograph each day of something that *used* to be important, but now has no has value for you. It may be easy to take photos of things that are no longer important in your life, but bear in mind two things as you pick your subject:

- The thing, person, or place you pick must once have been important to you or of personal value in some way.
- The actual things you photograph are really *symbols* of things that have changed. For instance, photographing your briefcase may represent the idea that it's no longer important to place all your personal meaning in a job or career.

1. Think of things, places, or people that you were once important, but are of little value in your present life. List up to ten things that were important once, but are unimportant now:

a. _____   f. _____

b. _____   g. _____

c. _____   h. _____

d. _____   i. _____

e. _____   j. _____

2. For each day, think of something that used to be important, but isn't anymore. Use the list you just created to help, or just let things wash over you as the day passes, staying open to whatever comes up that day. Take just one photo each day.

3. Complete each day's entry with a description of the photo you took. After you've completed the entire week's worth of photos, develop them and return to complete the entry.

DAY 1

Day: _____ Date: _____

a. What did you photograph today? _____

b. Why was this your choice? _____

c. Why did it used to be important? _____

d. Why is it no longer important? _____

e. What does this change symbolize? _____

f. Will it become important again? _____

g. What does this change in importance say about you? _____

_____

DAY 2

Day: _____ Date: _____

a. What did you photograph today? _____

b. Why was this your choice? _____

c. Why did it used to be important? _____

d. Why is it no longer important? _____

e. What does this change symbolize?_____

f. Will it become important again?_____

g. What does this change in importance say about you?_____

_____

DAY 3

Day: _____ Date: _____

a. What did you photograph today? _____

b. Why was this your choice? _____

c. Why did it used to be important?_____

d. Why is it no longer important?_____

e. What does this change symbolize?_____

f. Will it become important again?_____

g. What does this change in importance say about you?_____

_____

DAY 4

Day: _____ Date: _____

a. What did you photograph today? _____

b. Why was this your choice? _____

c. Why did it used to be important?_____

d. Why is it no longer important?_____

e. What does this change symbolize?_____

f. Will it become important again?_____

g. What does this change in importance say about you?_____

_____

DAY 5

Day: _____ Date: _____

a. What did you photograph today? _____

b. Why was this your choice? _____

c. Why did it used to be important? _____

d. Why is it no longer important? _____

e. What does this change symbolize? _____

f. Will it become important again? _____

g. What does this change in importance say about you? _____

_____

DAY 6

Day: _____ Date: _____

a. What did you photograph today? _____

b. Why was this your choice? _____

c. Why did it used to be important? _____

d. Why is it no longer important? _____

e. What does this change symbolize? _____

f. Will it become important again? _____

g. What does this change in importance say about you? _____

_____

4. After the six days are completed, get your film developed. Line up each photo into the order it was shot. Do you see any relationship between the things you photographed as now unimportant? Is there some obvious theme?

_____

_____

5. What has this journal entry helped you to focus on in your life?

_____

_____

_____

_____

6. How do these photos reflect a change in *you*?

_____

_____

_____

_____

THINGS TO THINK ABOUT

- How difficult was it for you to come up with things that were once important, but now have less value?
- What do these sort of changes in value say about you or your life at this time? Are the changes permanent?
- Do you like the changes in importance? Do you want some things to return to their former importance, and some things to remain changed?
- Is it important to realize that some things have become *un*important?

Putting *You* into Your Life

The last two entries helped you to think about your life and the things in it. But, like every other entry in this journal, the thing you're *really* writing about is *you*. In the final entry in this three-part series, you'll once again use a camera to capture something important in your life. You!

This is the essence of the self-portrait, which for hundreds of years has been the artist's way of looking directly at himself or herself, and describing something meaningful to others. What could be more familiar to you than your own face and your own life, and what could be more difficult to see differently? And what could be more interesting and important than exploring your own life?

The true self-portrait isn't simply a physical likeness; it is a representation of an emotional, intellectual, or spiritual reality. Whether purely realist (Rembrandt) or wildly abstract (Picasso), the self-portrait represents something important about the artist that, in many ways, represents the essence of that artist. The final journal entry in this series has you create a photographic self-portrait. But, even in the most straightforward scenario, you face many choices in creating the self-portrait. What pose should you take, from what angle will you shoot it, and in what sort of light? What will you wear? Will it be a close-up, and will be you be alone in the photo? If you include something else in the photo, will it be a person or a thing? Where will you shoot the photo?

In other words, a "simple" self-portrait becomes quite complex when your goal is to delve for something deeper than a pure likeness. Everything in that self-portrait adds some dimension to its meaning and representation of you.

For this journal entry, once again load your camera with film or buy a new disposable camera. Take at least one photograph each day, making each of them a self-portrait. Most likely the self-portrait will be of you, but the things in it (besides you) and the way the shot is taken become part of the self-portrait. Perhaps you'll even decide to take a shot of something or someone else that, in some way, represents you and can count as a self-portrait, even if you're not in it. Think creatively. At the end of each day, add an entry for that day, and complete the final entry at the end of the six days, after you've had the film developed.

One final note, there's more than one kind of self-portrait. Songs and poems are often self-portraits of a kind, and certainly autobiographies are always self-portraits. This whole journal is one form of self-portrait.

A "simple" self-portrait becomes quite complex when your goal is to delve for something deeper than a pure likeness.

A SELF-PORTRAIT

1. Complete a brief entry at the end of each day of this journaling exercise.

DAY 1

Day: _____ Date: _____

a. What you did learn about yourself today as you planned for and took your self-portrait?_____

_____

b. What was the most difficult part of shooting a self-portrait today?

_____

_____

c. Did you feel satisfied by the photo you took?

_____

_____

DAY 2

Day: _____ Date: _____

a. What you did learn about yourself today as you planned for and took your self-portrait?_____

_____

b. What was the most difficult part of shooting a self-portrait today?

_____

_____

c. Did you feel satisfied by the photo you took?

_____

_____

_____

DAY 3

Day: _____ Date: _____

a. What you did learn about yourself today as you planned for and took your self-portrait?_____

_____

b. What was the most difficult part of shooting a self-portrait today?

_____

_____

c. Did you feel satisfied by the photo you took?

_____

_____

DAY 4

Day: _____ Date: _____

a. What you did learn about yourself today as you planned for and took your self-portrait?_____

_____

b. What was the most difficult part of shooting a self-portrait today?

_____

_____

c. Did you feel satisfied by the photo you took?

_____

_____

DAY 5

Day: _____ Date: _____

a. What you did learn about yourself today as you planned for and took your self-portrait?_____

_____

b. What was the most difficult part of shooting a self-portrait today?

_____

_____

c. Did you feel satisfied by the photo you took?

_____

_____

DAY 6

Day: _____ Date: _____

a. What you did learn about yourself today as you planned for and took your self-portrait?_____

_____

b. What was the most difficult part of shooting a self-portrait today?

_____

_____

c. Did you feel satisfied by the photo you took?

_____

_____

2. After the six days are completed, get your film developed. Place the photographs next to one other, in the order in which they were shot. Look over each, starting with the first shot. Is there a theme apparent in the photos you took?

_____

_____

3. What do these photographs say about you?

_____

_____

_____

4. Did the type, style, look, or theme change over the six days?

_____

_____

_____

5. Which photograph is the least accurate, and why?

_____

_____

_____

6. Which self-portrait is the most accurate, and why?

_____

_____

_____

7. What did you learn about yourself during the course of the entry?

_____

_____

_____

_____

THINGS TO THINK ABOUT

- Can you frame your favorite self-portrait? Is there any reason you wouldn't?
- Has your self-portrait changed over the years? What would it have looked like ten years ago? What might it look like ten years from now?
- Is it important to change things in your life now so that your self-portrait in ten years is flattering?

Talking to Yourself

Perhaps nothing is so important as the internal dialogue. Your internal voice can be a guiding beacon or can hold you back; it can uplift you or condemn you. That inner voice can be self-affirming and fortifying, or it can offer up distorted messages about what is real and what is important (see the "Distortions in Thinking" journal entry in Chapter 7). This is conversation that goes on within you. It's an important conversation, because if you consciously tune in to it, it can help you stay in touch with your feelings and help you make decisions that will shape your life and relationships in the way you *want* them to be shaped.

That inner voice can be self-affirming and fortifying, or it can offer up distorted messages about what is real and what is important.

The next journal entry will help you to tune in to yourself for one full day. If you find the entry useful, use it repeatedly. You can use the entry daily for five straight days, or once each week for the next month, or every once in a while. Copy the blank entry if you think you might want to repeat it.

For the entry, you'll need a small notepad that you can carry around with you for the day. Write the following sentence starts down in your pad, and once every two hours (set your watch if you have a watch alarm), pull out your pad and finish them:

- *I'm thinking about . . .*
- *I realize that . . .*
- *My life would be emptier without . . .*
- *I don't want . . .*
- *I recognize the value of . . .*
- *I know I can . . .*
- *I'm feeling . . .*
- *What's important is . . .*

Take at least five minutes to complete them, longer if you'd like. Begin the entry when you first wake up, and make your last entry sometime in the evening. You should have at least seven entries by the end of the day. Sometime in the evening, read back through each of the entries in note pad and summarize your answers in the journal entry below.

TODAY

1. *Today I thought about . . .* _____

_____

2. *Today I realized that . . .* _____

_____

3. *Today I recognized that my life would be emptier without . . .* _____

_____

4. *Today I realized I don't want . . .* _____

_____

5. *Today I recognized the value of . . .* _____

_____

6. *Today I know I can . . .* _____

_____

7. *Today I'm feeling . . .* _____

_____

8. *Today what's important is . . .* _____

_____

9. *I hear an inside voice that says . . .* _____

_____

_____

_____

_____

- What *is* important in your life? Do you know?
- What sort of inside voice do you usually hear? Is it supportive and friendly, or critical and hostile?
- Do you ever think about this inside voice? Do you ever listen to it? Would it help to pay more attention to this inner dialogue?

Moving Forward with Fresh Eyes

If you've consecutively worked your way through *The Healing Journey Through Job Loss,* by now the sting of your job loss is moving into the past. As you make decisions about the rest of your life, it'll be important to do so with clear thinking and fresh ideas, many of which, ironically, will be based on what you've learned from losing your job. Are you able to use the past to plan and build your future?

CHECKPOINT: NEW THINKING

1. What have you discovered about yourself?

_____

_____

_____

2. What have you discovered about your life?

_____

_____

_____

3. What's important in your life now and ahead?

_____

_____

_____

4. What changes do you see ahead?

_____

_____

_____

5. What needs to get left behind?

_____

_____

_____

6. Where do you go from here?

_____

_____

_____

THINGS TO THINK ABOUT

- Is looking inside something that can help your decision-making process? Do you need to find ways or the time to be more contemplative?
- How can you best use new eyes and apply fresh ideas in thinking about and planning your future?

14

Destination:
HEALTH AND WELLNESS

"A sound mind in a sound body is a short but full description of a happy state in this world."
—JOHN LOCKE

PATSY

My parents always talked about health being the most important thing. Of course I heard it, but it never really meant anything to me. After being out of work for weeks, I realized my health was going down the tubes. I actually didn't realize it until a friend told me how lousy I looked.

I thought about that when I went home. I realized that I'd been much more sedentary since being out of work and had been feeling pretty much under the weather emotionally. My diet was poor as I'd given myself permission to eat any junk food I wanted, and I didn't have the interest or the energy to take good care of myself. All in all, I realized the irony of having all this time to do just that—take care of myself in every sense of the expression—yet here I was letting myself get run into the ground. All because I wasn't working. I realized that I had the chance to get back to some of the things I always said I didn't have time for. I realized that my folks were right: "If you don't have your health, you don't have anything."

THIS IS A time when people in the United States are becoming far more health conscious and aware of their weight, diet, and general fitness. Nevertheless, despite a growing awareness of public-health issues, many people are still far from healthy, whether physically, emotionally, or spiritually. The United States remains a country with many health issues, from weight, diet, and physical fitness to substance abuse, suicidal tendencies, and crime. In fact, the very emphasis on diet programs, home health equipment, personal fitness, nutrition, and smoking cessation, and the growing awareness of depression, suicide prevention, and the personal and public costs of alcoholism and drug abuse, illustrates this point.

Wellness represents the idea that health cuts across all areas of your life. Health is a matter of a sound mind and a sound spirit in a sound body.

When we speak about health, it's easy to think first of the body. However, it's difficult to be physically healthy when you're depressed or anxious, and mental health issues often lead to problems with physical health. Wellness represents the idea that health cuts across all areas of your life. Health is a matter of a sound mind and sound spirit in a sound body. In this context, as defined by the World Health Organization, health is not simply the absence of illness, but also a state of physical, mental, and social well-being.

Your Health

Ironically, at the time that your emotional health needs to be optimal and that you have the time to develop or maintain physical health, the issues in your life may be sending you in exactly the opposite direction. Not surprisingly, job loss and prolonged unemployment more often lead to feeling debilitated and devitalized as opposed to exhilarated and rejuvenated. Unemployed people can become quite distracted and overwhelmed by their feelings, thoughts, and concerns, and fall into routines of poor health that may include poor diet, lack of exercise, and, at the extreme, patterns of substance abuse and depression.

Yet, of course, it's always important to stay in good shape. It's especially important while you're both looking for new work and thinking about and redefining your life. You want to feel good and think clearly while undertaking such an important search and making decisions that may affect you for years to come. Although it's difficult to say *exactly* what you should be doing for your physical, mental, and spiritual health, we *can* say with relative certainty that there are ten things you can do that will help you to stay healthy:

Unemployed people can become quite distracted and overwhelmed by their feelings, thoughts, and concerns, and fall into routines of poor health that may include poor diet, lack of exercise, and, at the extreme, patterns of substance abuse and depression.

- Don't smoke.

- Limit your use of alcohol.

- Limit your salt intake.

- Limit and monitor your intake of saturated fats and cholesterol.

- Eat adequate amounts of fiber, fruits, and vegetables.

- Watch your diet for other excesses that may be unhealthy in large quantities.

- Keep your body weight within the normal limits for your height, build, and age.

- Get regular exercise, four to five times weekly.

- Find ways to relax and reduce stress.

- Remain active with friends and in the community.

These ten things come together to define wellness as a *combination* of different types of healthy activities. Taking care of yourself in this way not only helps invigorate you, but fosters your ability to stay on top of things and think clearly. Use the next journal entry to look at your health and your health practices.

A MAP FOR HEALTH

1. Think about each of the ten health areas defined above. They reflect basic tasks in remaining physically, emotionally, and spiritually healthy.

2. Think about how well you manage each area, and use the checklist below to rate yourself. Next to each area, circle the number that most best describes this area is a health issue for you or how well you're managing each area.

- A score of 1 indicates that this area is not a health concern for you at all (for instance, perhaps you don't smoke in the first place), or you're well on top of the health issue (perhaps you've cut out smoking completely).

- At the other end of the scale, a 4 means that you either indulge in clearly unhealthy behaviors (you eat loads of heavy fat foods or drink alcohol heavily, for example), or you never think about your health practices in this particular area (you don't pay any attention to what you eat, or simply drink as much as you want whenever you want, without giving it a second thought).

Ten Healthy Practices	No problem at all.	I watch this carefully.	I try but not very hard.	I pay no attention to this at all.
Don't smoke	1	2	3	4
Limit use of alcohol	1	2	3	4
Limit salt intake	1	2	3	4
Limit saturated fats/cholesterol	1	2	3	4
Adequate fiber/fruits/vegetables	1	2	3	4
Avoid excesses of unhealthy foods	1	2	3	4
Body weight within limits	1	2	3	4
Regular exercise, four to five times weekly	1	2	3	4
Relax and reduce stress	1	2	3	4
Active with friends and community	1	2	3	4

3. Reviewing your answers to Question 2, are there any areas of your health that require some attention?

_____

_____

_____

4. If you see health problems or concerns, do they tend to fall in all three areas of body, mind, and spirit, or just in one or two?

_____

_____

_____

5. What can you do to improve your health in any or all three areas of wellness?

_____

_____

_____

6. What *will* you do?

_____

_____

_____

THINGS TO THINK ABOUT

- Do you ever think of your physical or emotional health as a problem or concern? Even if you don't, are there other people in your life who express concern about your health?
- Do you take care of your body or neglect it? Are you satisfied with your overall health, or should you be considering making a change in the way you think about your health?
- Does it make sense to think of health as body, mind, and spirit? What does this mean to you?

Finding Time to Breathe

Breathing and relaxation exercises can change both physical and mental states—affecting brain wave patterns and helping to relax muscles—and can even influence your capacity to learn.

One thing that job loss *has* given you, even if you've never actually taken the opportunity, is room to breathe. Beyond the metaphor of getting breathing room, it's quite *literally* important to use this room to breathe. Breathing and relaxation exercises can change both physical and mental states—affecting brain wave patterns and helping to relax muscles—and can even influence your capacity to learn. Most people, understandably, take breathing for granted; it's just something we do. They rarely take the time to breathe deeply, and, consequently, their lung capacity is never fully used, nor their blood fully oxygenated. Deep breathing and breath control exercises are recommended by dozens of health books, health training programs, and spiritual disciplines, such as yoga, as a key to relaxation, meditation, and wellness. Take some time now to breathe deeply and completely, and then complete the following journal entry.

Take five deep breaths. Clear your mind and let it wander while breathing, and physically and mentally relax for about five minutes before completing your entry. The relaxation is as important as the deep breathing that precedes it. Complete the entry in this relaxed state of mind. As this is an exercise that you might want to repeat, copy the blank entry before using it for the first time.

A BREATH OF LIFE

1. Take your breaths; then continue to relax for at least five minutes. Describe the experience.

_____

_____

_____

_____

2. *Breathing this way makes me feel . . .* _____

_____

_____

3. *With each breath, I . . .* _____

_____

_____

4. What thoughts or feelings ran through your mind as you breathed?

_____

_____

_____

5. What thoughts or feelings ran through your mind as you relaxed after the breathing exercise?

_____

_____

6. *Breathing this way opens me up to . . .* _____

_____

_____

7. *Breathing this way symbolizes my journey by . . .* _____

_____

_____

THINGS TO THINK ABOUT

- Do you usually stop to breathe deeply during your day? If not, what was it like to concentrate in this way, shutting out the things that perhaps normally distract you from your own body?
- Is this an entry worth repeating, perhaps even daily?
- What can deep breathing teach you about personal health care?

Managing Stress

Stress is an unavoidable part of life. The world is a stressful place. Crowds are stressful. Being a parent is stressful. The evening news is stressful. Being laid off or fired is definitely stressful, and remaining unemployed only increases stress. Stress, then, goes with the territory. The questions are: how do you manage unavoidable stress, and how do you reduce it whenever you can?

Stress is actually a great vehicle for talking about the relationship of mind and body when it comes to health. Stress often upsets us emotionally, and it can also can lead to or significantly contribute to real physical conditions such as heart attacks. The way we manage and deal with stress is often critical to our ability to function effectively, and under extreme conditions people can suffer from severe stress disorders, such as post-traumatic stress disorder, that can effectively ruin their lives if not treated.

Stress often upsets us emotionally, and it can also lead to or significantly contribute to real physical conditions such as heart attacks.

The ability to manage stress then, and to "unwind," is an important tool for both physical and mental health. Of course, there are as many ways to relax as there are people. For some, relaxation comes naturally, whereas others have to learn *how* to relax. Relaxation can be as simple as switching off your mind and letting your body go loose, or it can include any number of actual relaxation activities.

There are also, unfortunately, plenty of people who *try* to relax by heavy drinking, drug use, or overeating (or undereating). This is a road many have trodden with poor success. If you're having trouble learning to relax, or if you are depending upon alcohol, drugs, medications, or food to help you, get some help. It's very important to discuss the issues with your primary care physician or professional counselor, not only to help find ways to successfully relax, but also to ensure that you're not in the process of developing some major habits that will only serve to increase your problems and your level of stress.

Use the following journal entry to think about your physical health and how it's affecting you: your energy, your ability to take care of things, and your mood. If you've kept in good physical shape, the journal entry may allow you to simply reflect upon the importance of good health. The ability to relax is very important to good physical and mental health. To put it another way, the *inability* to relax carries a big price tag: physical and emotional fatigue, tension and stress, worry and anxiety, and a constant state of being on edge.

The ability to relax is very important to good physical and mental health.

PHYSICAL HEALTH AND RELAXATION

1. Is taking care of yourself physically a problem? What kind of shape were you in when you lost your job, and what kind of shape are you in now?

_____

_____

_____

_____

2. Which areas of your physical health concern you the most? Have these become concerns only recently, or have they always been a source of concern?

_____

_____

_____

_____

3. Have you been able to physically relax since your job loss? What most prevents you from being able to relax?

_____

_____

_____

_____

4. How do you relax? What techniques might help if you used them? In addition to the items on the checklist, add others that can or do help. Add your use of alcohol or drugs, prescribed or over-the-counter medications, or other things you do to help relax, even if you're depending on ways to relax that are self-destructive or otherwise potentially harmful. Be honest.

__ breathing control   __ cup of tea   __ exercise   __ meditation

__ quiet music   __ reading   __ relaxation tapes   __ self-hypnosis

__ sports   __ talking   __ television   __ visualization

__ walking   __ warm bath   __ writing   __ yoga

other: _____   _____

_____   _____

_____   _____

5. Look back at the items you just checked off. Are any of your preferred ways to relax problematic?

_____

_____

_____

_____

6. What can you do to learn to relax more completely?

_____

_____

_____

_____

7. What can you do to ensure that you're taking care of your physical health?

_____

_____

_____

_____

8. How do you see the relationship between physical health and mental health?

_____

_____

_____

_____

9. What are the greatest areas of stress in your life right now?

_____

_____

_____

_____

THINGS TO THINK ABOUT

- Is relaxing a problem for you? What most interferes with your ability to relax? How can you overcome these obstacles?
- Do others ever express a concern that you don't relax enough or that you relax in ways that are unhealthy?
- Do you need to change some aspect of your lifestyle in order to take better care of your health?

Take a Hike

One of the easiest and best methods for exercising body, mind, and soul all at the same time requires no special equipment, sophisticated techniques, or membership fees. Walking is something you do just by stepping outdoors.

Walking every day can tone up your muscles, help you lose weight, get your heart and lungs moving, and improve your overall health. But, of course, there's several versions of the walk. There's the slow and meditative stroll, the cross-country ramble, the brisk hike, and the power walk. Each exercises different parts of your body, mind, and soul, and each is equally valuable. Where one type of walk may be purely for quiet pleasure, another kind may be to return to nature or get out among other people. Still another may be for pure exercise, and yet another to clear your mind. Any way you go, walking is for life and health. Consider taking a walk several times each week, if not every day. Walk your dog, stroll with your partner or your children, take a lunch break and hike to a lake, get out among the crowds in the city streets.

For the final entry in this chapter, take a walk. Any kind will do. Make sure you take your mind along as well. This walk will exercise your senses as well as your body. This walk is designed to get you in touch with your health and your sense of wellness, in addition to the things around you. By opening your mind and using your senses to let things in, you exercise your spirit as well. Read the entry blank before you leave for your walk, or take it along with you. Get familiar with the questions posed by the entry, and take a notebook with you. Periodically stop, think about the questions asked, and jot down your thoughts, experiences, and ideas in your notebook. Write your journal entry immediately after completing your walk, while the walk, its ideas, and the energy it's given you are still fresh in your mind and your body. This is another entry to be used again and again, so consider copying the blank before using it for the first time.

WALKING WITH YOUR MIND

1. What kind of walk did you take today?

_____

_____

_____

_____

2. Describe your walk.

_____

_____

_____

_____

I walked along . . . _____

_____

I walked through . . . _____

_____

Along the way, I . . . _____

_____

3. What did you notice that you'd never noticed before?

_____

_____

_____

4. What smells did you most notice?

_____

_____

_____

5. What colors stood out the most for you, and why?

_____

_____

_____

6. What sounds could you pick out, near and far?

_____

_____

7. What interesting textures did you stop and feel?

_____

_____

8. What did you see of special interest?

_____

_____

9. What did you think about on your walk?

_____

_____

THINGS TO THINK ABOUT

- Did you choose to walk alone or with someone else? Why? How would your walk have been different had you chosen differently?
- How did you most benefit from this walk? Were there any downsides?
- Will you keep walking? Either way, what prompts your choice?

Checkpoint: Staying Healthy

"Life is not living, but living in health."
—MARTIAL

It's too easy in the best of times to not take care of yourself. It's even easier, under difficult circumstances, to let your mind, body, and spirit get run into the ground. There are endless reasons to stay healthy—for yourself, for your family, for your future.

Bear in mind those ten points for staying healthy. Are you watching over and taking care of your physical health? Is your emotional health okay? Are you connected to a community of people and ideas that keeps your spirits high? If the answer to each of these questions is "yes," then you're in prime shape to move on. You have wellness. If the answer to any of the questions is no, you need to think carefully about the things you must do to preserve and improve your health and well being. Your job loss is behind you now. Your future is right ahead.

15

Blueprinting the Future

STU

Years ago, I happened to be in a library that housed the autobiographies of Harvard graduates. As I read the autobiographies, I was struck by how many of the authors described a transformation in their lives. They described a period of stress, followed by a return to family, to nature, and to relationships. At first I thought it might have to do with their ages, but then I noticed that the books I'd picked up were from the years just after the Great Depression. The transforming events these people were talking about were business failures, economic disasters, job loss, and bankruptcy. My vision of the Great Depression had been a vision of bread lines and of stockbrokers jumping out of windows to their death, yet here were people talking about it as if it had been the best thing that had happened to them.

Years later, I spent my free time as a volunteer physician for a loose network of rural communes. I'd grown up in a city, so, for me, seeing people living without electricity, growing their own food, and taking care of their own lives in this way was like walking out of a tunnel into the sunlight. It gave me a vision of the range of ways that one could live. The lives of many of these commune dwellers were richer and more exciting than the lives of my peers with their fancy cars, televisions, and apartments.

IF YOU'VE CONSECUTIVELY worked your way through *The Healing Journey Through Job Loss,* it's taken you a while to get this far. You've worked through some difficult experiences and times, but by now you're at the far end of your journey, well into the final stage of decision making and self-renewal. At this point, your tasks really do involve learning from the past, leaving it behind, and moving into your future—fresh, more wise, and with a renewed spirit and energy.

If you're not feeling this way, perhaps you need to think more about some of the tasks involved in the earlier stages. Perhaps you've moved through this book too quickly, and haven't really worked through earlier tasks or addressed and resolved earlier issues. If you still find yourself overwhelmed with feelings about job loss or are really suffering from self-doubt, consider reworking earlier chapters. If you're still struggling with financial issues or haven't developed a financial plan that works for you, you're probably not ready for the work involved in moving ahead.

The clear goal in this final destination chapter is a look into the future. As the old saying puts it, "Today is the first day of the rest of your life."

The Transforming Power of the Present

Sometimes things happen that can change our lives if we let them. By this point, you may even be feeling that this life-*shattering* event can be a life-*changing* event. Perhaps you're already in the process of transformation. Transformation, like everything else, runs along a continuum. At one end it can be volcanic, changing the face of everything in its path. At the other end, transformation can be subtle—more evident in the way you think and feel than in pure action.

Transformation, like everything else, runs along a continuum. At one end it can be volcanic, changing the face of everything in its path. At the other end, transformation can be subtle—more evident in the way you think and feel than in pure action.

For some people, getting fired or laid off is an inconvenience, an interruption, an annoyance. For others, it's a disaster, a destructive event, the start of a downward spiral from which they struggle to recover. For some people, however, being laid off is a transforming experience that, despite its traumatic and anxiety-provoking components, leads to the most positive changes in their lives. The best possible outcome of this difficult journey is that your job loss can be turned into a positive and transforming experience.

What can you carry into the future with you from your job loss and all it's taught you? The ability to draw from your past and use it as a source of comfort and strength is a task required of us all, but perhaps most clearly marks the point at which you leave the *recovery* part of your work behind and focus entirely on *rebuilding* and stepping out into your future. Another piece of this same idea is that those who haven't learned from the past risk repeating mistakes. It's been said that insanity is doing the same things over and over while expecting the outcome to be different.

Part of moving on is letting go, an enormously difficult task for many people. Failing to let go of an anchor can pull you down with it, and holding on to a lead weight can keep you from rising to the top. Transformation goes one step beyond that, where you use your past to *change* your future. As you think about the past, consider all it's given you, not all it may have taken.

Before you complete your next entry, think about the words of the English poet, Ben Johnson: "He knows not his own strength that hath not met adversity."

The ability to draw from your past and use it as a source of comfort and strength clearly marks the point at which you leave the recovery part of your work behind and focus entirely on rebuilding and stepping out into your future.

TRANSFORMING THE PAST

1. What has your job loss taught you about your life?

_____

_____

_____

2. What has your job loss taught you about the place of work in your life?

_____

_____

_____

_____

3. What has your job loss taught you about what's important to you?

_____

_____

_____

_____

4. What has your job loss taught you about yourself?

_____

_____

_____

_____

_____

5. Complete these sentences.

a. *Job loss has been fertile ground for me because* . . . _____

_____

b. *My job loss has allowed me to* . . . _____

_____

c. *Following job loss, I've come to most appreciate* . . . _____

_____

d. *Following job loss, I've come to most regret* . . . _____

_____

6. In what ways has job loss transformed you?

_____

_____

_____

_____

7. Where do you most want to go from here?

_____

_____

_____

_____

THINGS TO THINK ABOUT

- Are you ready to move with your future? Do you need to do more decision making and reflective work before making major life decisions?
- Are you ready and able to let go of feelings that will only drag you and keep you down? If not, where and how can you get some help in learning how to let go?
- What does "letting go" mean to you? Is it the same as forgiving or forgetting, or is it a different concept?

Preparing for the Future

The future isn't a singular thing. It's an array of alternatives and a container of possibilities. When you create a blueprint for your future, you're mapping out ideas and a plan for your *own* future, not the future of the world at large. But, as you consider your future, you must take into account the possible future of the world around you in which your own future will play out. For instance, the development of the talking motion picture meant bankruptcy for any silent movie studio that hadn't considered this future.

When you create a blueprint for your future, you're mapping ideas and a plan for your own future, not the future of the world at large.

Blueprinting the future is always hard, but it is essential, especially in stormy times. Although predictions about the future are often wrong, thinking about the future is crucial. Even if your thinking isn't always accurate, as long as you attempt to integrate your thinking about the future with changes taking place in the present, you will move more smoothly into the next phase of your life.

As you plan ahead, conduct a SWOT analysis: strengths, weaknesses, opportunities, and threats. As you think about each element in this model, recognize that they are *not* to be treated or viewed as independent factors, but are intended to be linked together in a model of self- and market evaluation and direction setting. The SWOT analysis is often thought of as a *strategic* model that can help you see things in yourself and the work environment clearly, so you can plan specific ways (strategies) to get where you want to be.

The SWOT analysis is often thought of as a strategic model that can help you see things in yourself and the work environment clearly, so you can plan specific ways (strategies) to get where you want to be.

- What are your *strengths*? How do these match with the field? Where do you want to be, and how will your strengths help you to get there?

- What are your *weaknesses* and limitations? Where do you fall short in the current, changing, and developing job market? Where do you want to be, and what personal or professional limitations will you have to overcome?

- What *opportunities* are there out there? What does the field have to offer you, and where is the market going? What allies and advantages exist out there that can help you to meet opportunities and accomplish goals as you develop them?

- What are the *threats* to your career and your decisions? What sort of competition is out there, and where do you fall short of being able to meet these challenges? What might disrupt or interfere with your ability to recognize, seize, and build upon opportunities?

The message here is basically clear: get to know yourself, your field, and know the environment and climate in which you and your professional field meet.

1. *Take personal charge of your career.* Don't wait for someone else to change the course of your life, either by firing you or creating new opportunities for you.

2. *Recognize your weaknesses and limitations.* Understand the sorts of skills that your field requires, and spot where your current skills, attitudes, and knowledge fall short, not only with respect to your own profession, but similar professions as well.

3. *Build new skills and expand your capacity.* Identify the broad range of specific and general skills that fit both your own profession and extend to other relevant professions as well.

4. *Sharpen your people skills and your communication skills.* These are those interpersonal skills that help you to understand and be understood, and will always help you not only find or create work, but succeed in every endeavor. Virtually every endeavor involves interpersonal communication.

5. *Look at what's out there, and train yourself to spot opportunities.* Research your field, or others that interest you, and keep a close eye on other marketplace and social changes that might affect or influence your field.

6. *Recognize change.* Some people don't see change coming, until they trip over it. Even then, they may see the fall as the result of their own clumsiness rather than change itself. Recognizing change is one of the keys that allows you to make the changes in yourself that will keep you in the game.

7. *Be flexible.* How can you stay in a changing game without being flexible and having the ability to adapt to change? This is a simple, but often difficult, task.

Understand the sorts of skills that your field requires, and spot where your current skills, attitudes, and knowledge fall short, not only with respect to your own profession, but similar professions as well.

*Don't limit yourself to
what you do now.
Think about spreading
in new directions,
stretching yourself
further, or even going
entirely outside of your
current profession.*

8. *Understand and befriend new technologies.* A pencil was once a technological breakthrough. Although people think of technology as electronic "high-tech," technology extends to virtually anything that helps you do your job. Find ways to understand the technologies that affect your work choices instead of becoming intimidated, frustrated, angered, or fearful of them.

9. *Don't limit yourself.* Don't limit yourself to what you do now. Think about spreading in new directions, stretching yourself further, or even going entirely outside of your current profession. Expand your horizon, and become a futurist.

SWOTing YOURSELF

1. In what ways are you taking personal responsibility for your career?

_____

_____

_____

_____

2. Describe up to ten weaknesses or limitations that are or might affect your ability to get to where you want to be.

_____   _____

_____   _____

_____   _____

_____   _____

_____   _____

3. Describe up to ten new or expanded skills that will enlarge your capacity to meet the needs of your current profession or provide opportunities in new fields.

_____   _____

_____   _____

_____   _____

_____   _____

_____   _____

4. Are your interpersonal and communication skills where they need to be? Why or why not?

_____

_____

_____

_____

5. Are you tuned in to the opportunities in the workplace? If so, how can you take advantage of this knowledge? If not, what do you need to do in order to become more aware?

_____

_____

_____

_____

6. In keeping with Question 5, are you aware of changes in your field or the larger market or social environment that are, or might be, important to consider as you think about and plan your future?

_____

_____

_____

_____

7. Where do you have the greatest difficulties in adapting to meet the changing work environment?

_____

_____

_____

_____

8. Is technology your friend? If not, do you want to overcome this obstacle? If so, how can you best use technology to your advantage?

_____

_____

_____

_____

9. Are you thinking big enough? Is your imagination hard at work as you think about your future?

_____

_____

_____

_____

THINGS TO THINK ABOUT

- How do you feel you came out of your SWOT analysis? Are you heading in the right direction, or is your thinking more limited than you would like?
- Do you feel stuck? If so, do you need to get some professional help with career planning and development? If not, did your analysis give you the sort of information you need to strategically plan for your immediate and long-term future?
- Do you have the right attitude and skills for moving forward in this changing job market?

Making Decisions

If you completed Chapter 8 ("Destination: Managing Practical Matters"), you've worked on an action plan and understand the process of turning decisions into actions. Briefly, the process involved in arriving at a solution requires that you first *understand* the problem/issue, that you *develop* a goal/solution, and that you think through and identify the actual *steps* you're going to take to achieve that goal/solution. In short, you *first* recognize that there's a problem or issues of some kind to be resolved, and you *then* decide how you're going to solve it.

You can see that before implementing an action plan, you must *first* have made a decision. It's this *decision* that the action plan aims to bring into *reality*. For instance, you may have decided to sell your home, move to Salt Lake City, and buy a new home. Your action plan will determine the steps you take to sell your home, locate another, and move, but the decision came first. *Before* you can implement a solution, you *first* have to develop the decision.

Accordingly, it's important to have a way to consider your choices, think them through, and have a process through which you can develop and arrive at well-considered decisions. No matter what the decision, it's always valuable to have a decision-making process. The more important the decision, the more important it is to have a decision-making process. Of course, there are many different kinds of decisions, from the very concrete (I'm going to sell my house and move to Utah) to the very vague (such as decisions to simply experiment with an idea.) In fact, there's really no such thing as a "nondecision"; even a decision to *not* decide is a decision. Despite the fact that decisions are an inevitable fact of life, the range of scenarios in which decisions are required falls between compulsory and optional.

Before *you can implement a solution, you* first *have to develop the decision.*

Sometimes, you *must* make a concrete decision. You have to decide if you want to keep living in that house before the mortgage comes due or a decision will be made for you (foreclosure). You have to pay child support if you're a divorced noncustodial parent. Other decision situations are optional, situations where you don't have to make a decision right now, or perhaps ever. You may not *have* to change your lifestyle, the car you drive, or where you live. The decisions you face fall into one of these two primary categories, or somewhere in between.

Either way, compulsory or optional, you're usually faced with some choice in decision making—if not in the actual decision itself then in how you implement the decision. Making life more complicated, there's often more than one "correct" decision and more than one "wrong" choice. Here's where it's especially valuable to have a guide to decision making that can help you to think about and arrive at—not the "right" decision—but an *appropriate* decision.

Break your list of possible decisions into those that are really unrealistic at this time and those that are within the realm of possibility.

- *Recognize that you have choices in the first place.* Most of the time, you're not simply a victim of the way things "have" to be.

- *Consider the nature of the problem that you're trying to resolve.* Every decision is a *response* to a particular situation: what is the issue, problem, or situation you need to address?

- *Think of all the possible choices you have.* In brainstorming, the goal is to simply list every possible choice, including the outlandish ones. In this step, your job is to be creative—what decisions *could* be made?

- *List the rational and realistic choices.* Break your list of possible decisions into those that are really unrealistic at this time and those that are within the realm of possibility.

- *Evaluate your choices.* Now think about the possible decisions that you can realistically make. Which ones most fit the particular circumstances of the problem you're trying to resolve, and which ones most fit the circumstances of your present life? If only one choice comes up, you may even come up with a clear decision at this point.

- *Consequences.* What are the downsides to your possible choices? Who will be affected by your choice, and how? How will your choices affect your life, your finances, your relationships, and so on?

- *Reflection.* Think about the decision you're planning to make: What will it feel like to actually take those steps and make that choice? What will it feel like to *not* make that choice? Is the decision you're pondering permanent or is it reversible?

Think about the decision you're planning to make: What will it feel like to actually take those steps and make that choice? What will it feel like to not make that choice?

The next journal entry will help you think about individual decision choices, as well your decision-making style in general. Copy the blank format if you think you may want to repeat the entry. Follow the general model for decision making described above. This is a framework you can use to think about and map out solutions for almost any issue in your life, from relationship choices to decisions about changes in your lifestyle.

MAKING DECISIONS

1. Briefly describe one decision you're currently pondering:

_____

_____

2. Name at least six different choices for resolving this issue.

_____   _____

_____   _____

_____   _____

3. Review the possible choices you've just identified, and select the three most rational and realistic choices. Under each, describe how this choice could fit the circumstances and reality of your life.

a. *This solution fits because* . . . _____

b. *This solution fits because* . . . _____

c. *This solution fits because* . . . _____

4. Now select just one of these choices, and use it as the focal point for the remainder of this entry. You might want to repeat this entry several times in order to think through each of the possible choices you identified. _____

5. What are possible consequences of this choice? Is there a price to pay?

_____

_____

_____

_____

_____

6. How will your life be affected by this choice?

_____

_____

_____

_____

_____

7. Who else's life will be affected by this decision, and how?

_____

_____

_____

_____

_____

- Do you better understand the issues and choices involved in this decision? What stops you from making a choice and acting on it in this case?
- Can you afford to take a chance on this decision, or are the consequences irreversible?
- Are you acting too quickly on decisions, or are you not acting quickly enough?

Activities Yet to Come

Your blueprint for the future will never really be complete, because your future is always just ahead. One reason to think about your future in this way is to ensure you have a map that can both help you survey the terrain and help you figure out how to reach your goals.

Use the next entry to tie your future to your past. By writing about important past projects, you have the opportunity to think about what sort of tasks or activities are meaningful to you. By thinking about your *past* life in this way, you can get valuable clues to what you want in your *future* life.

This is a freewriting entry in which you will write one paragraph about important projects completed at distinct points in your life and development. As you write about each project, dating back to your elementary school years, think about *why* it was important or meaningful to you, and if this activity contributed to a sense of personal success or growth. Once you've written about each project, consider what patterns or links exist between each project, and what they say about the sort of things that are important to you in your work. Use these past experiences to help think about and realize what's important in activities yet to come.

Feel free to go beyond the space provided in the entry below, and write on a separate sheet of paper or in a separate journal you may have been keeping. In that case, use the space in the entry to provide a summary of each project and its importance.

MESSAGES FROM THE PAST

1. Write about an important project or activity from your elementary school years.

_____

_____

_____

_____

_____

_____

_____

2. Now write about an important project from your middle school years.

_____

_____

_____

_____

_____

_____

_____

3. Describe an important or meaningful project or activity from high school.

_____

_____

_____

_____

_____

_____

_____

4. If you went to college, write about an important college project. If not, write about an important project from your early work life.

_____

_____

_____

_____

_____

_____

_____

5. Pick one more activity or project that was important in your life, after college or in your later work life.

_____

_____

_____

_____

_____

_____

_____

6. Review each project you've described. What did they have in common? Is there a pattern of some kind that made these important or meaningful to you?

_____

_____

_____

_____

_____

_____

7. Now pick a project or activity with an unsatisfactory outcome. Write about what made the outcome disappointing or less than satisfactory, and what might have led to a different outcome.

_____

_____

_____

_____

_____

_____

_____

8. Why was failed project an important experience?

_____

_____

_____

_____

_____

_____

9. What will you need in your next job or career to feel good about that future?

_____

_____

_____

_____

_____

_____

Passion, People, Places, and Posterity

It's usually true that we work to earn money. But if we work *only* to earn money, we're shortchanging both ourselves and our employers.

As you move on in your work life, think about the four *P*'s:

- *Passion*. Doing what you love to do.

- *Place*. Finding a work place that utilizes your talents and supports your creativity.

- *People*. Working with a team of coworkers who share your goals.

- *Posterity*. Remembering what you wish to leave behind, in your work and in your life.

Checkpoint: Moving On

As you near the end of this chapter, you near the end of this part of your life journey. Some decisions are behind you, others are imminent, and others far ahead. Your recovery and rebuilding work has helped you deal with the emotional, practical, and personal issues that you've faced since losing your job. These are the very skills you'll need in every facet of your life as you move forward, and it will be important for you to use the skills you've learned along this journey as you deal with future issues. And, of course, the future is here *now*. Many of these issues are likely to be present in your life *today,* or clearly pending.

There are many resources available to help you deal with the practical, emotional, and other very real issues of job loss, unemployment, and career development. These include self-help materials such as books and videotapes, motivational and practical seminars that deal with financial planning and small business development, Internet exploration and contacts, and face-to-face work with outplacement counselors and career specialists. In fact, there are countless resources, all designed to help you figure out your life in every detail and from every possible angle.

If you've found your job loss journal to be useful, return to it often. As issues, feelings, questions, and problems emerge over time, turn to your journal as a source of quiet reflection and personal development. Use the final entry in this final chapter to think about this journey, where you've come from, where it's taken you, and where it may yet lead.

As issues, feelings, questions, and problems emerge over time, turn to your journal as a source of quiet reflection and personal development.

REFLECTIONS ON YOUR JOURNEY

1. *I've most learned* . . . _____

_____

_____

_____

_____

_____

_____

_____

_____

_____

_____

2. As I look back on my recovery and rebuilding work, I . . . _____

_____

_____

_____

_____

_____

3. My job loss journey has left me feeling . . . _____

_____

_____

_____

_____

_____

_____

4. The most bitter part of my journey has been . . . _____

_____

_____

_____

_____

_____

_____

5. The best part of my journey has been . . . _____

_____

_____

_____

_____

_____

_____

6. I most need to say . . . _____

_____

_____

_____

_____

_____

_____

THINGS TO THINK ABOUT

- Has this entry helped you realize you're ready to complete your recovery work or that you still have a way to go before you're ready to leave your job loss issues behind?
- What will it take for you to really feel that the issues, anxieties, and fears raised by losing your job are resolved? Will those feelings ever go away?
- What has this journey most taught you about yourself, and your life in general?

16

As One Journey Ends, Another Begins

IT'S DIFFICULT TO say when any journey *really* ends. The end can be defined as reaching a specific destination, but in life there's always another destination. Journaling work, for instance, is never really over unless you consciously decide to never write again. And there is no clearly defined end point for dealing with the sort of issues raised by job loss and unemployment, from the practical to the emotional. Yet here you are at the end of this journal and, accordingly, this part of your journey.

As you reach this point, you've only completed one step in a lifelong journey. What you've been through and what you've learned through your journaling work sets the pace for the journey that's ahead. If your encounter with job loss has left you emotionally intact, then you're in good shape for the things that are yet to come. That which doesn't harm you only makes you stronger. If your work with job loss has offered enlightenment, fostered personal growth, and even enriched your life, then all the better.

If your journey has left you emotionally shaky and uncertain, consider getting help. There are many sources of assistance, in-

There is no clearly defined end point for dealing with the sort of issues raised by job loss and unemployment, from the practical to the emotional.

cluding individual counseling and job loss and outplacement support groups. This sort of help is not only for those who continue to feel the devitalizing impact of job loss grief. You don't have to be experiencing emotional difficulties to get help dealing with unresolved issues, uncertainties, and life decisions. Individual counseling provides a useful and, for many, an important place to explore life issues. Support groups offer a cooperative, communal, and sensitive environment for sharing and interacting with others in similar situations. These sort of helping environments offer a great deal for a great many people.

Where will your life take you now? If you've used your job loss journal through this difficult time, then you've no doubt found it useful, and it may have served many purposes—a place to express or explore feelings, or both; a guide to help direct you through job loss and help shape your decisions; a narrative of your life in troubling times; a mirror to reflect your relationships and interactions with others; a means of learning new ways to see yourself and the world around you. If you've come this far in *The Healing Journey Through Job Loss,* then you've found value in the journaling process. Will your journal continue to be a useful tool and valuable companion as you continue along your journey?

If you've found the entries in this journal useful, you may want to explore *The Healing Journey* or *The Healing Journey for Couples*. Both of these books provide more general journal-writing exercises that are focused on self-exploration and personal growth. There are also other Healing Journey books in this series focused on specific issues such as grief, divorce, and the menopausal passage.

MY JOURNAL

1. How has your journal been most useful?

_____

_____

_____

_____

2. Have certain types of journal entries been more useful than others? Which ones?

_____

_____

_____

3. What's been the most difficult aspect of journaling for you?

_____

_____

_____

_____

4. What's been the most fulfilling aspect of journaling?

_____

_____

_____

_____

5. Overall, describe your experience keeping this journal.

_____

_____

_____

_____

6. My journal . . . _____

_____

_____

_____

_____

_____

_____

_____

_____

_____

_____

_____

_____

THINGS TO THINK ABOUT

- Have you enjoyed keeping a journal? If you've kept a journal before, what was different about this journal?
- Will you continue to use a journal in the future? If so, will you only keep a journal under special circumstances, or will you keep a daily journal?

In completing this book you've accomplished a great deal, and you've taken important and significant steps down the path to healing, self-help, and personal growth. Although your journey will never be complete, but instead is a process, the lessons and methods learned in this book will help you along the way.

Where will you go next on your healing journey? What tools or people will you need to help take you further along that path?

About the Authors

PHIL RICH, EdD, MSW, holds a doctorate in applied behavioral and organizational studies, and is a clinical social worker diplomate with a master's degree in social work. Over the past two decades he has worked as a director of treatment programs, a clinical supervisor, and a practicing therapist in both the outpatient and inpatient setting. He currently maintains a private outpatient practice in western Massachusetts, in addition to his position as a program director. He is the lead author and editor of the Healing Journey series.

STUART A. COPANS, MD, is a board-certified child psychiatrist and an associate professor of clinical psychiatry at Dartmouth Medical School. He practiced psychiatry at the Brattleboro Retreat for over twenty years, currently serves as a consulting psychiatrist, and maintains an active outpatient private practice. He is the author of numerous books on psychotherapy and substance abuse, is trained in art therapy, and frequently makes use of both written and graphic assignments in his work with patients.

KENNETH COPANS, CPA, has been a practicing accountant in Newburgh, New York, for 30 years, as well as practicing in New Jersey and South Carolina. He is a member of the New York State Society of Certified Public Accountants and the American Institute of Certified Public Accountants, and has lectured extensively on financial planning and personal finances.

Acknowledgments

OUR GREAT APPRECIATION always to Kelly Franklin, the Publisher at John Wiley and the directing influence behind the Healing Journey series. Kelly is wonderful to work with and has made all of these journeys possible. Many thanks also to Sasha Kintzler, the Associate Managing Editor at Wiley who ensures the quality of this series. Much appreciation also goes to Dorothy Lin, our Associate Editor who provided editorial assistance and editing skills for this book. We must also acknowledge the reason for this book, and those many people whose lives have been turned upside down by job loss.

FROM PHIL: In addition to those acknowledgments above, my gratitude and appreciation goes to Stu, who has been my coauthor and partner on three of these journeys and was the energetic spark that got this whole thing going. Stu and I have spent many hours discussing our own work and the workplace environment in general. A special thanks and note of constant appreciation for my wife, Bev, who is an active supporter, great listener, capable reviewer, good friend, and great love in my life, and has patiently (and anxiously) watched me go through many job changes. Finally, my gratitude for having a daughter like Kaye, who is a gifted and bright light in my life, and a wonderful reason to keep working through life's journeys.

FROM STU: As always, working with Phil has been a pleasure. He helps me keep up the pace and look at things in new and helpful ways. Special thanks to Mary for her support as I have explored my own job changes, and to Ken, whose financial wisdom has informed both me and this book. Also to Laurie, Roy, Jon, and Ben, who have all embarked on their own exciting journeys of employment.

FROM KEN: To Phil and Stu who have shown me the more emotional side of job loss. To JoEllen, Rich, and Mark, who have suffered through many tax seasons and whose support enables me to keep the same job, as painful as it may be at times. And to the staff in my office, without whose aid my job would be impossible.